Dirac and
Other Essays
on
Economics.

Henry Daniel Vera
Ramirez.

HENRY DANIEL VERA RAMIREZ.

DIRAC AND OTHER ESSAYS ON ECONOMICS.

With much affection for *Vicky*

***Ivanda* and *Jacobo*.**

CONTENTS

LIST OF FIGURES

LIST OF TABLES

PREFACE

The first chapter focuses on the importance of investment in Latin American countries as a strategy to achieve better levels of innovative incorporation in internal production processes. The document considers it fundamental to analyze the situation of these countries in relation to state and private investment, recognizing that innovation is a complex but significant element in the progress towards overcoming social obstacles such as poverty and the distribution of wealth. The document focuses on making a methodological proposal to analyze some variables, which can be measured by the small productive units, as well as in the approach to a model that describes the relationship between some key factors in each of the countries and in the export of goods with high technological incorporation, which suppose, in addition, incorporation of investment in innovation.

The preponderance that MSMEs have currently acquired, as a preferential framework for the economic development of nations and, above all, of the so-called emerging nations, is evidenced by the fact that they have increased significantly in terms of their quantity in the last two decades. On the other hand, it is evident that its growth has also been supported by significant increases at the population level, the impossibility for large companies to support the growing number of people who are part of the labor market and for repeated policies that seek to strengthen entrepreneurship as a mechanism of cohesion and development. It is for this reason that the increase of MSMEs has generated a relevant debate regarding its impact on development, the generation of surpluses that sustain its functioning, the tax burden to which they are exposed, the costs both fixed and variable in which they incur and ultimately their sustainability over time.

Besides this, it is supremely important to recognize the fact that many aspects influence each of them, and these have to do with the sector of production of goods and / or services in which they are located, as well as financial aspects such as: capital, its cash flow, its net worth, its level of production and the macroeconomic atmosphere in which it operates. In this set of relationships, it is necessary to distinguish between a set of concepts that in principle could mean the same and that ultimately refer to different stages of development of MSMEs: *small and medium industry, operational unit, productive unit, small and medium-sized company, microenterprise[1], among others[2]*. The move to new production

---

[1] A microenterprise is an association of people who, operating in an organized manner, use their knowledge and resources: human, material, economic and technological, for the production of products and / or services provided to consumers, obtaining a large margin of utility after covering its fixed costs, variable costs and manufacturing expenses (Monteros, 2005, p.12).

units that are currently observed, implies the need to build a model that seeks to integrate them into a competitive space that results in the favoring of their particular needs and especially their contribution to the economic development of the country, from concepts basic as the technological incorporation to the productive processes and of the innovation in products and services.

Taking into account these conceptual differences, this document proposes a model that involves technological, financial and equipment elements that allow the MSMEs to be able to sustain itself in a markedly competitive market in the long term and that takes into account some of the theories they deal with microeconomics, to generate more efficient levels of production, incorporating technology, capital and work.
In this sense, the contribution of production functions such as Cobb-Douglas, originally enunciated in Cobb & Douglas (1928), developed in León (1967) and empirically reviewed in Sánchez (2013), together with the theory of capacity technique in relation to the factors of Deslandes (1975) and the traditional theory of costs in Blair & Kenny (1983), Horngreen (1991), Polimeni et al., (1989) and Varian (1996), provide important elements that contribute to the construction of the present proposal. In the first part of the chapter, the evolution of MSMEs from the family business is discussed, followed by a review of their access to financing and credit; subsequently, the relationship between production and capacity is theoretically addressed, followed by a theoretical review of the exogenous elements that affect MSMEs. The following part explores the construction of a model from Carvajal (2002), which considers the multifactorial coefficients of capital and labor, to later specify the same with all intervening variables and analyze their relevance. Finally, a set of conclusions are provided.

The following work tries to make an approach between two disciplines: physics and economics, since the application of the preliminaries proposed by physics from the approaches of Paul Dirac (1928). Then we try to apply the determinant of the matrices obtained by the physicist to an interaction of two classic productive factors: capital and labor, but not before reviewing the main production functions that have analyzed this relationship. Finally, the application of the determinant is exposed to analyze the location of eleven countries in relation to their productive factors. It is considered that the application of the determinant can be constituted as an element of analysis to observe the behavior of the interaction between these productive factors in different countries. The Dirac´s preliminaries are an example of divergent thought, which can explain the relation between productive factors in different countries. Further, this issue will be a quantitative measure for the study of development in the small and median enterprises or productive

---

[2] Zerda & Rincón (1998), emphasize the need to differentiate diverse concepts such as informal sector, microenterprise, small and medium enterprises, a difference that in its concept does not perform the traditional analysis when referring to these as biases of the neoclassical school.

units. The analysis in the paper uses the software *STATA 11*, to obtain the results and propose the discussion.

Portfolio theory in their contributions from the point of view of Markowitz (1952), Sharpe (1970), Tobin (1958), have become fundamental analysis for understanding the investment from the point in view of the uncertainty and more from the point of view of risk. Diversification, for example, that in principle is recognized as fundamental to reducing the risk of portfolio element has become a paradigmatic theory starting from a Bayesian probabilistic view. This document aims to make a brief analysis of the theoretical foundations, from the point of view of mathematical statistics of the main models of portfolio emphasizing proposed by Markowitz and an application from a portfolio of three shares of market listed in Colombia during the period between January 2016 and July 2016

Among his works Paul Adrian Maurice Dirac (*1902 †1984), is also recognized for his support with the so-called Dirac Delta function DDF. The present document intends to articulate the usefulness of this function and analyze of the behavior of the shares in the stock market. One may assume that in a daily share price, there may be some *impulse events*, which will describe specific behavior in discrete periods in a normal or traditional trading market, and the mathematical development of its function, may constitute a tool for the analysis of these motions.

The first chapter was published in the book Social Entrepreneurship, Innovation as an engine of business growth, ISBN: 9789587633276 Editorial Uniminuto in the year 2019. The second chapter was published as a chapter in the book on Tools for MSMEs in Colombia ISBN: 9789587632637 Editorial Uniminuto in the year 2018.. The third chapter was published in the compilation book of the International Research Congress in Colombia ISBN: 9789585998261 Editorial TEINCO in the year 2019. The fourth chapter was published in Spanish in Spain 2018. Editorial EAE ISBN: 9786202110174. And the last chapter corresponds to the memories of the presentation of the paper on the Delta Function of Dirac the COLCAP index, made for the second CONGRESS OF INTERNATIONAL RESEARCH TEINCO REVOLUCION INDUSTRIAL 4.0 in 2019.

Acknowledgements.

I would like to begin by thanking the Corporación Universitaria Minuto de Dios, where I worked as a teacher, to Professors Cesar Aguirre, Felix Fernando Dueñas and Camilo Peña with whom I shared the area of economic research. Similarly, to the authorities of the Universidad Colegio Mayor de Cundinamarca of which I was a teacher and academic coordinator in the Faculty of Social Sciences, especially to the Dean of the Faculty, Professor Patricia Duque, and the faculty of the university.

Chapter 1

Incidence of investment in innovation policy in Latin American countries

Generally, when a study is made on investment in a country, the analysis of foreign investment and mainly of foreign direct investment (FDI) tends to be privileged, ignoring the flow of investments made by citizens within the country. nation. However, internal investment focused on innovation and technology is difficult to trace due to the same conditions of the historical conformation of the business sector and especially the overcrowding of medium and small businesses, as elements of economic development. It is, in practice, difficult to determine the flow of resources that a productive unit can effectively destine to strengthen innovative processes, even, in many cases, ignoring the same concept. On the other hand, it is found that the new tendencies of the production worldwide, suppose as a fundamental element the innovation in products and services, generating therefore an added value, that specifically for the case of the Latin American countries and particularly for Colombia, implies the need for increasingly high and significant investments in education and in research and development.

During the last decades, and especially in accordance with the approaches of several of the development models, three aspects were considered as main elements of economic progress: industrialization, poverty reduction and the adoption of hard and soft technology in the productive sector and mainly in the small-scale productive sector, or the productive sector that has been constituted by small productive units.

It could be argued that there have been significant advances in the three aspects referenced above, but little by little the issue of innovation has been introduced in discussions on development and policy makers have seen the need for these aspects to be accompanied by a new trend that involves a fairly broad concept of innovation, a concept that at first seemed to be located in a gray and unclear space, while generating an interesting and irresolute debate: what is innovation?. Not in vain, innovation has emerged as a very important element in the definition of science and technology policy in several Latin American countries. This, despite the little investment in education that can result in a slow improvement in the processes of incorporation at a technological and innovative level in the countries of the area.

This document, therefore, intends to analyze the relationship between investment in innovation in Latin American countries, as a strategy to progress efficiently in the objectives that are raised internally and interregional: poverty reduction, incorporation of benefit to the production and collective welfare. If innovation is the spearhead of science and technology processes, how much have aspects related to innovation-oriented investment contributed to Latin America. On the other hand, it is important to establish which policies and actions have had a positive effect on the development of science and technology within Latin American countries, which, as successful experiences, can be replicated with their own adaptations in other contexts and in other countries of the region. Region. For example, in some countries, such as Colombia, state institutions responsible for promoting and designing policies aimed at scientific development and innovation have generated strategies such as tax benefits for those institutions and productive units that seek to introduce innovative elements in their productive process. . In this regard, Crespi, Fernández, & Stein, (2014), consider that tax incentives for Research and Development can be useful tools, since they are broad spectrum in their application and do not address a very specific business focus, contemplating most of the economic sectors that range from MSMEs to large corporations.

Taking into account this set of preliminary ideas, the structure of the document starts from the consideration of the scope and incidence of investment in some Latin American countries, followed by some global trends in the face of the incorporation of innovative investment in some specific sectors. Later, in a second section a direct analysis is made about the relationship between investment and innovation. In a third part, the presentation of some indicators that can guide the small productive units in the follow-up of the innovative investment based on four basic elements: financial area, customers, internal processes, and learning / growth. Finally, a model is proposed that allows an empirical and quantitative analysis of the relationship between internal production, export of goods with high technological value and direct foreign investment, to analyze the current situation of our countries in relation to this investment (see Appendix A).

Conceptualization of the innovation process

It is important to recognize that the process of innovation, from an economic perspective, owes its initial position to the approaches of Schumpeter (1947), emphasizing the importance of the implementation of new processes and the creation of new products. However, this is not restricted to the case of creating only new products, but to the form of to perform them in a new way. The creation of new products and services means that new processes and new products materialize a set of learning that is essential for innovation. In recent decades, and especially since what has been called the post-capitalist era, emphasis has been placed on the importance of innovation in processes related to areas such as commercial, financial and in general in the services sector, which, if While they do not directly imply the enjoyment or enjoyment of a good or product, they guarantee that they will satisfy the multiple human needs. There is, therefore, a direct relationship between knowledge and innovation. The innovative process must be considered as a marginal element of creation and transformation of the raw material, input or productive factor in a final product, or a process of transformation of knowledge in a service.

Innovation, then, is a complex process that involves the transformation of that knowledge for the benefit of the company for productive improvement. From an approach that we can consider close to the approaches of Bertalanffy (1968), for Kline and Rosenberg (1986), innovation supposes non-linearity, non-automaticity and non-systematicity. His proposal a systemic approach contemplate the following elements:

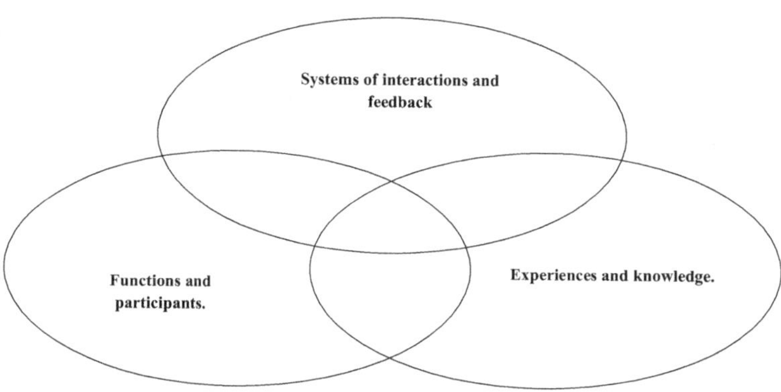

Figure 1 Aspects related to Innovation. Source: Elements of innovation. Own construction on the data of Kline and Rosenberg (1998) and Malaver and Vargas (2004).

These three elements integrate the following approaches: empiricists (importance of experience), systemic (flows within structures) and a functionalist approach, which refers to the importance of the roles and roles of economic actors. It is also important to recognize the relationship between experience as a source of knowledge that is considered as an aspect related to any innovative process and which implies that the productive sector in the maturity that currently characterizes the levels of production developed introduce the collection of that experience in innovative ideas.

On the other hand, Bravo (2012), in relation to the concept of innovation, - following the Oslo Manual (2006) -, considers that innovation can be framed in two large groups: an innovation related to marketing and another with the so-called innovation organizational the definition provided by the manual is as follows:

Innovation is the introduction of a new or significantly improved product (good or service) of a new marketing method or a new organizational method, in the internal practices of the company, the organization of the workplace or external relations (Manual from Oslo, 2006, p.146).

Innovation, from this point of view, could be very restrictive, if only these two aspects are considered. The current trend in innovation has been influenced by different ideas that range from conceptions that consider innovation as an aspect based on creativity to another series of theories, which have been influenced, among other forms of thought, by evolutionism and they have emphasized the consideration that only those productive units and / or companies that incorporate creative elements in the production of goods and services survive.

It can be affirmed that the evolutionism in Economy, is oriented to analyze that the companies in their evolution act like rational agents avoiding the genetic fatalism, which leads towards its disappearance. Rationality implies the desire to maintain and locate itself in a proper and appropriate market niche that allows further development. For this reason, the innovation in principle would be related to the technology within the firm, but in turn, the technological redoubts that are gradually overcome as economies of scale are achieved. Another aspect is related to market conditions that will influence two fundamental elements for innovation: the speed of technological change and its orientation (Álvarez and García, 2012).

Authors such as Di Maio (2003), support a basic idea that has to do with the relationship between the rate of scientific progress and the emergence of new ideas in relation to technological progress. However, it happens that innovations often appear, but are not appropriate, and this depends on the second aspect mentioned in the previous section: the structure and condition of the market, or if you want, if the innovation is relevant to the structure of the market. Alternatively, for the level of development of it. In addition, a basic element comes into play and is the learning that is obtained through the accumulation of experience during the production process. Learning, then, is a primordial element, which, in turn, cannot be analyzed, without considering the following characteristics: irreducibility, non-transferability and progressivity.

Álvarez and García (2012), affirm the existence of three learnings:

• Throughout the Research and Development process.

• Through the design and manufacture of goods or the design of the provision of services and

• Throughout the use of the product by the final consumer.

Other authors such as Nelson and Winter (1982) have emphasized the role of routine. Routines tend to present in organisms, structures that often determine behavior, but that can undoubtedly be a trap for innovative processes. On the one hand, if the routine is not capitalized in terms of accumulation of experience and, on the other hand, if it makes the structure of the firm rigid or inflexible, the routine will not contribute in any sense to the innovative culture.

Developing countries face contradictory situations, since they have to build policies focused on innovation processes, under a scheme of external technological transfers, (generally do not create their own technology), creating in turn a culture of imitation and invention appears, but in the form of invention in the midst of scarcity. This bases a fundamental aspect and is that, in many contexts of lack, tends to analyze the set of innovative processes because of the needs and shortcomings of the contexts. This is contradictory, since, as shown below, the results of the GII-2018 innovation index, the much more advanced and better-income society's lead innovative processes and it is not precisely the contexts of scarcity that lead globally. This element is another trap that must be taken into account as a preponderant aspect for the innovation policy and for access to investment resources for its implementation.

Relationship between investment and innovation

According to the Kruger Corporation (2017), there are only three countries in the world that have managed to exceed 3% of the total value of their GDP, invested in development and research: South Korea, Israel and Japan. The registration for Latin America is even more worrisome, while Brazil is the only country that approaches 1%.

If we look more specifically at the analysis of Latin American countries, we find that the situation is bad. At low levels of income, exists low investment in research and development that results in a low export of products with high technology incorporation.

The data suggest that, within the Latin American countries, the export of goods with high technological value, under the assumption that significant investments in innovative processes will generate an increase in said exports, is led by countries such as Argentina, Colombia and Ecuador that present an important relevance in the area, compared to countries with lower levels such as Mexico.

Although investment in this sector has always been accompanied by the participation of the government budget, it is important to mention that in many countries investment is also made based on capital flows from abroad. Mainly, investments from other countries can contribute to the generation of an innovation investment process, especially in the private sector. However, it could be stated in principle that this investment occurs in areas of high-income levels, which have identified key sectors for the generation of innovative strategies.

In this sense, the country that leads foreign direct investment is Brazil, with a significant difference compared to the total number of countries in the area. The rest of the countries present a similar and close behavior for the period corresponding to the years 2010-2015. On the other hand, a relationship can be found between the gross domestic product GDP, for each of the countries shown in the following graph, which places Chile and Uruguay as the countries with the best income levels (GDP) per capita. For the years referenced above and as will be seen below, investment in innovative processes:

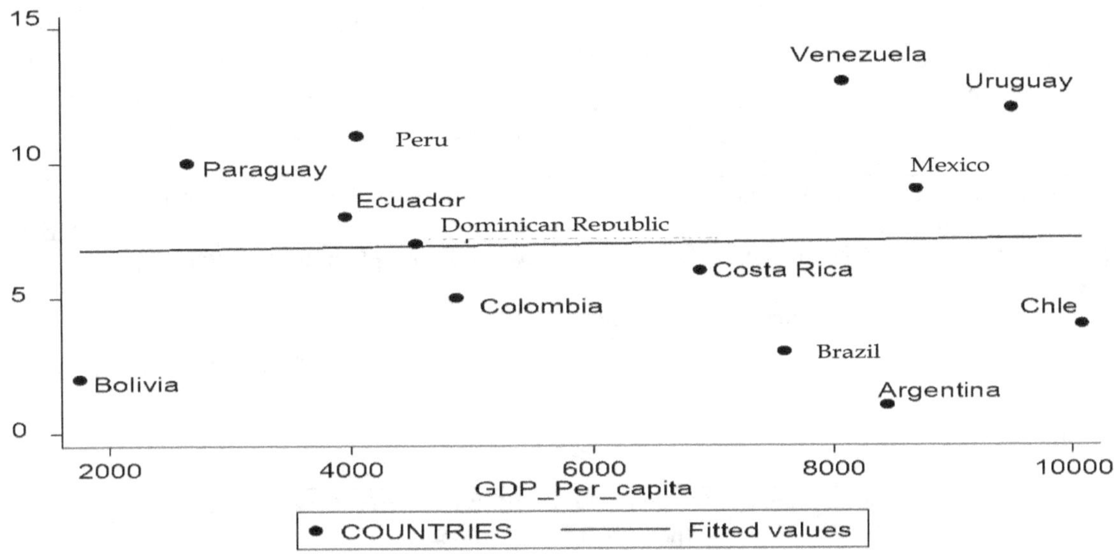

Figure 2 Average Gross Domestic Product per capita 2000-2015). Source: Own construction on the World Bank data (2015).

Later, in this document, we analyze how a relationship can be established between variables such as: exports in high technology products, investment flows, -mainly direct foreign-, and GDP per capita. Without these elements: greater investment, not only state but private innovation, compared to improvements in national income will not be able to improve export levels of products with high level of technological incorporation, which will slow innovative policy initiatives. Next, some global trends will be analyzed with respect to the innovation theme.

Some global trends

The report document on innovation published by the Global Innovation Index (GII-2018), locates, for the year 2018, a set of indicators (80), which try to establish a Rankin in front of the process of incorporation of innovation in the world. Undoubtedly, European countries are still the best placed, without ignoring significant advances in other areas that are making an important transition in the face of the imperative need to introduce elements that encourage innovation and, in particular, in the event of non-existence. , believe and implement public policies against innovative production processes. Worldwide, the following trend is observed:

Global Leaders	Leaders North America	Europe	Middle and middle east.	South America and the Caribbean.	North and West of Africa.	Far East and Oceania.	Sub-Saharan Africa.
Switzerland	United States.	Switzerland.	India.	Chile.	Israel.	Singapore.	South Africa.
Netherland.		Netherland	Iran.	Costa Rica,	Cyprus.	South Korea.	
Sweden.	Canada.	Sweden.	Kazakhstan.	Mexico.	Arab Emirates.	Japan.	Mauricio.
UK.							Kenya.
Singapore.							

Table 1 Leadership in Innovation at the Global Level GII-2018. Source: Own construction on the Global Innovation Index 2018 data

Although the trend shows European countries with important levels of industrialization and technological progress, it is worth highlighting, however, the advances in countries such as Iran, Kazakhstan in the Middle East. In sub-Saharan Africa: Kenya and Mauritius; Cyprus in the north-west of the same continent. It is evident that, in South America, the leadership has fallen to Chile and Central America, Costa Rica and Mexico. With respect to a division that relates countries in terms of advances in innovation vs. income, the following leadership map is obtained:

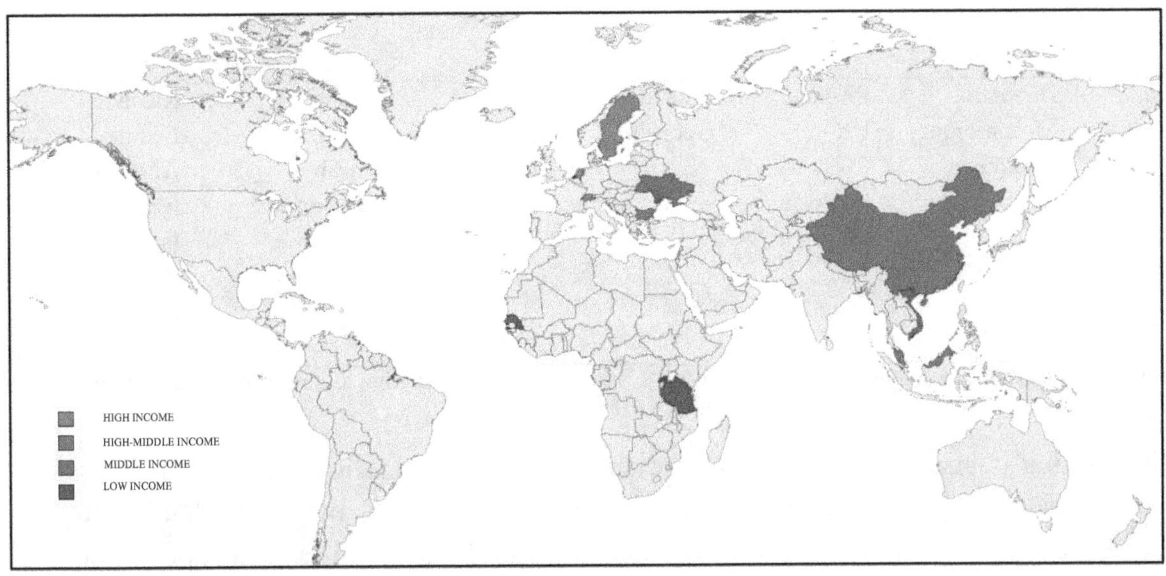

Figure 3 Leading countries in Innovation vs income level GII-2018. Source: Own construction on the Global Innovation Index 2018 data.

Among the high-income countries is again the global leaders: Switzerland, the Netherlands and Sweden. With respect to the high-middle income countries, there are China, Malaysia, and Bulgaria; while in the middle-income countries are Ukraine, Vietnam, and Moldova. The countries with low incomes and which are better ranked are Tanzania, Senegal, and Rwanda.

Other important elements that allow observing the presence of Colombia, have to do with the division carried out by the GII-2018, between countries that have achieved an important level of advances in innovation by dividing these advances into seven different categories, namely: creativity, infrastructure, knowledge and technology, institutional improvement, market sophistication, business and human capital sophistication and research. In the following table, you can see some countries that lead these categories of analysis:

Creativity	Infrastructure	Knowledge and technology	Institutions	Sophistication of the market	Sophistication in Business	Human Capital and Research
China. Turkey. Kenya. Mexico. Lithuania.	Denmark. Mozambique. Sri Lanka.	Sweden. UK. Costa Rica. Botswana Malaysia. India.	Singapore. Georgia.	Colombia. Japan. France.	Ecuador. Switzerland. Arab Emirates. Vietnam. Hungary.	Rwanda. Estonia. Australia. Iran. Israel. South Korea. U.S.

Table 2 Leadership by category of analysis GII-2018. Source: Own construction on the Global Innovation Index 2018 data

If this ranking is analyzed, in terms of the subcategories, the following characteristics can be seen: China excels in innovation in commercial brands by origin, Turkey in industrial design, Kenya in advertising and media, Mexico in export goods and Lithuania in creation of mobile apps. Denmark excels in ICT, Mozambique in capital investment in infrastructure, Sri Lanka in clean energy. Sweden is a leader in patents, while the United Kingdom is a scientific publication. Costa Rica in productivity growth, Botswana in creation of new business units. Malaysia in export of technological goods and India in sale of services applied to ICTs. Singapore is a leader in the regulation and quality of its institutions, while Georgia leads aspects related to the ease of starting a business (lower requirements). Ecuador leads the offer of companies offering formal training, Switzerland in university cooperation for industrial research; Arab Emirates in the development of clusters, Vietnam in the import of technological goods and Hungary in foreign direct investment (FDI).

Rwanda has global influence in educational institutions led by non-governmental organizations, Estonia in training in academic areas such as reading and mathematics, Australia in number of university students in higher education, Iran in graduates in science and engineering, Israel in number of researchers, South Korea in further expansion of the culture of research and development and the United States as universities. Colombia is referenced as a nation with relatively easy access to credit. This ranking represents a substantial improvement in aspects related to innovation issues and based on these aspects some basic ideas can be concluded: the best located are those countries that have high income, but this is not a condition to lead the ranking, either by area or by category, because many countries that do not really have high incomes lead in aspects related to the advance and innovation in categories complementary to innovation, which implies a wide field for the countries in these aspects and that constitutes a space of exploitation of market niches linked to these processes. Equally, one might ask, if these categories, do not suppose euphemisms, in the development of true integral strategies of innovation, especially in low-income countries and if their inclusion, does not obey only an insertion that really has nothing to do with novation it is itself. In the following table, we have the locations of the ten (10) main countries and the location of the best ones in Latin America and Central America:

Countries	Score/100	Place in the ranking
Switzerland	68,4	1
Holland	63,32	2
Sweden	63,08	3
UK	60,13	4
Singapore	59,83	5
U. S	59,81	6
Finland	59,63	7
Denmark	58,39	8
Germany	58,03	9
Ireland	57,19	10
Latin America and Central America	Score/100	Place in the ranking
Chile	37,79	47
Costa Rica	35,72	54
Mexico	35,34	56
Uruguay	34,2	62
Colombia	33,78	63

Table 3 Ten first positions and main Latin American countries GII-2018. Source: Own construction on the Global Innovation Index 2018 data

Next, we find the ten (10) countries that lead the ranking worldwide:

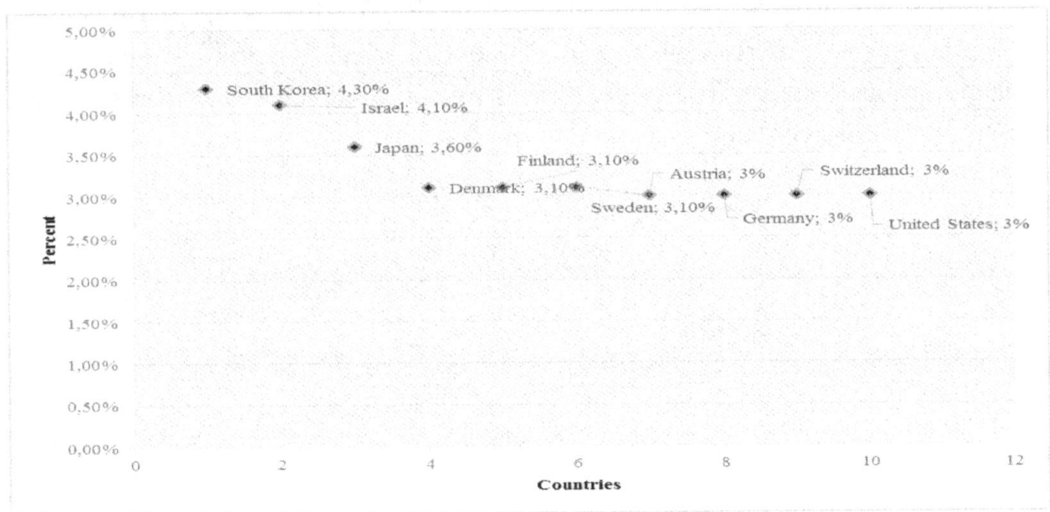

Figure 4 Ten first positions GII-2018. Source: Own construction on the Global Innovation Index 2018 data.

In addition, at the level of the countries in the area, we have the following data:

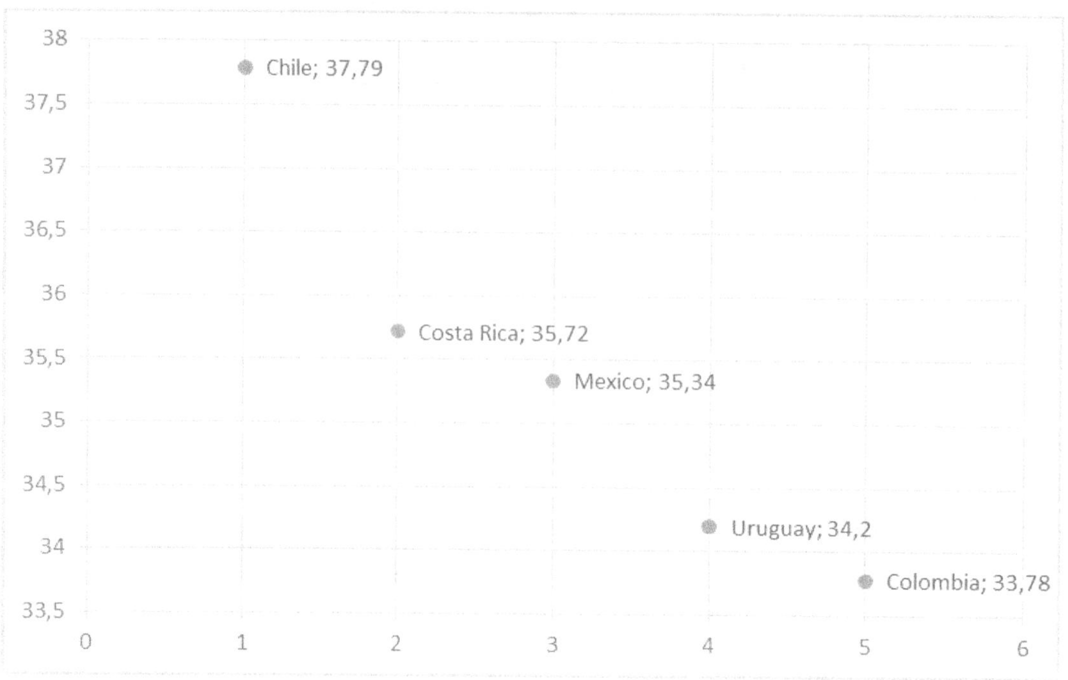

Figure 5 Location of major Latin American countries in GII-2018.Source: Own construction on the Global Innovation Index 2018 data.

Latin America and investment tied to Education

As noted above, the leadership in the area is evidenced by the advances in countries of Central America: Mexico and Costa Rica and in South America, Chile. This would be worth comparing with the investment made by these countries and, in general, the Latin American countries in education as a percentage of GDP. The following graph shows the relationship between the percentages of investment in education and the total GDP (Gross Domestic Product) in the different countries of Latin America. You can see low rates of investment in most of them:

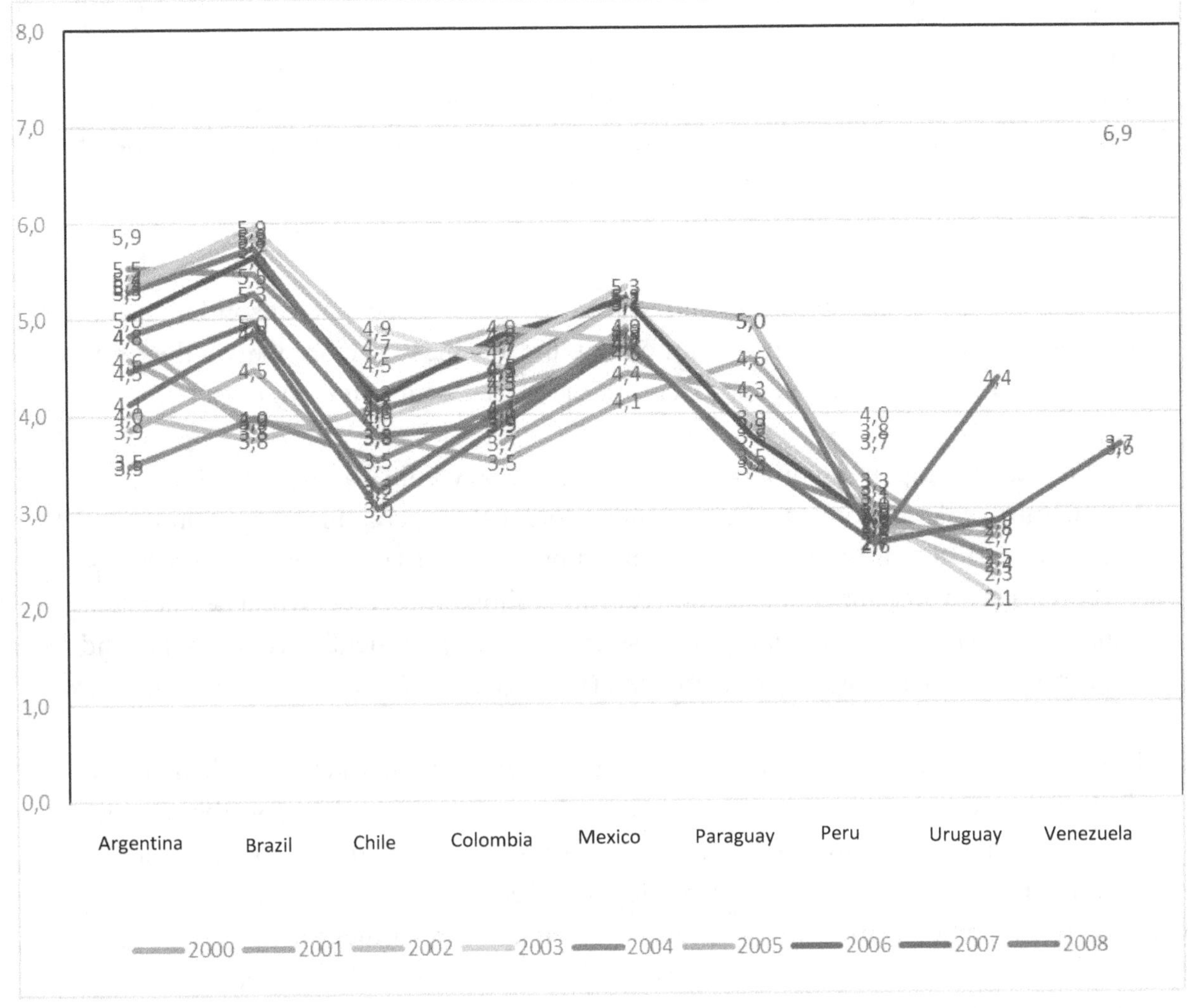

Figure 6 Investment in education as a percentage of GDP 2000-2016. Source: Own construction on the data of ECLAC (2018).

A significant increase can be observed in countries such as Brazil, followed by Mexico and Argentina with percentages that approach 5% of the total gross domestic product. Colombia has maintained investment levels in education between 3.5% and 5%. The lowest observed for the area are found in Peru and Venezuela. This aspect is often discouraging, considering that, in many countries in the area, innovation policies are mainly related to budgets in education. This does not mean that the incentives only come from the State, since the private company also carries out an important task in terms of supporting the introduction of elements that motivate innovative aspects in the production and sale of services.

The IDB (2010) in its report on science, technology and innovation, considers that, in Latin America, the areas of action in which innovation policy has been developed have been: *i)* supply-oriented policies; *ii)* demand-oriented policies and *iii)* policies oriented towards coordination strategies and methods.

The first, in the sense proposed by Buchanan (1968), would be oriented towards the creation and supply of public goods that allow the different social sectors to develop innovative processes through them. It is interesting here to analyze, as elements related to human development, the competences developed in the scientific field, and from a Keynesian perspective, infrastructure can be considered, despite their differences in terms of being intangible and the first tangible. Last, public goods themselves.

On the other hand, demand-oriented policies would be focused on consolidating and favoring the conditions for the development of the business sector, which therefore includes the entire entrepreneurial approach. As the same document recognizes:

> Entrepreneurship is an important factor for the vitality of industries and the dynamism of economies. The dynamic process of creating new companies contributes to introducing and spreading innovative products, processes, services, and organizational structures throughout the economy. The fact that new companies are a significant source of employment, productivity and economic growth is widely documented (IDB, 2010, p.57).

The last area of action is oriented to the need to carry out market, technical, legal, organizational, administrative and financial studies, which account for the design, implementation and evaluation of programs that are mainly aimed at economic sectors that integrate new production into their production. Technologies and that are generally expressed in groups of companies, - tendency to division, regardless of their size. The approaches can be substitutable, but really, so that the process of incorporation of the innovation can occur, its internal complementarity must be taken into account. The IDB (2010) considers it important to recognize that strategies for innovation in different countries have a certain emphasis that we could divide as follows:

Innovation strategies	Countries.
Diversification of innovation policy mechanisms.	Argentina Brazil Chile Mexico Uruguay.
They concentrate only on one strategy	Dominican Republic Guatemala Costa Rica.

Table 4 Innovation Strategies. Source: Own elaboration on IDB data (2010)

The IDB also insists that many countries have few instruments that focus on more strategic and selective actions. This has allowed that in some countries we can effectively speak of innovation policy, while in others the internal conditions weaken the possibility of advancing in the consolidation of the policy.

Anderson (2017) refers to the importance that innovations must have a spectrum of impact on a large scale. When referring specifically to the education sector, in some cases the large scale refers to the attention of changes in the structures and the allocation of resources, which can occur with a political will, but cannot generate a fundamental change in innovation but it works in the micro, complementing this action with state actions. In this sense, according to your proposal, you can think of two important categories to implement the innovations: on the one hand, adoption and implementation of changes, which must be developed and carried out by the central authorities in a system, which involves the direct and indirect action of the State and, on the other hand, the concentration in programs of local origin, which we could assimilate as local economic zones, whose innovative models can be replicated in other zones and productive units. The author considers that it is more relevant to concentrate on the second category, at the micro level, as an inductive strategy to consolidate innovation policy in the educational field.

The diagnosis carried out for our country by COLCIENCIAS, on research and development and that is condensed in document 1602 on Actors of the National System of Science, Technology and Innovation (2016), recognizes that the key points for the implementation of the Technology policy in our country focus on:

• Low funding for Science, Technology, and Innovation activities.
• Emphasis of the National Science, Technology, and Innovation Policy in the generation of knowledge.
• Weak prioritization of the sector in the country's policies.
• Implicit and discontinuous guidelines for the centers.
• Support infrastructure to be consolidated.

These considerations coincide, in many cases, with the situation previously presented in low-income countries with respect to internal investment policies in education, development, science and technology and particularly in innovation. In Colombia, within the framework of public policy, we can see how COLCIENCIAS has generated in recent years a series of documents that have tried to give support for action to the policy of technological incorporation in our country. The following table gives some of them with some comments regarding their scope and limitations.

Politics	Objective	Comments
CONPES 3834: Policy Guidelines to stimulate private investment in science, technology and innovation through tax deductions.	The general objective is to establish the policy guidelines, criteria and conditions that promote the effective use of the tax benefit of deduction for investment or donation in CTeI projects (science, technology and innovation), with the purpose of increasing private investment in activities of CTeI and the competitiveness of the productive sector.	This is the key document, which focuses on granting benefits to the productive sector that implements processes of incorporation of science and technology.
Policy of Actors of the National System of Science, Technology, and Innovation - SNCTeI.	The policy of SNCTeI actors (national system of science, technology and innovation) aims to promote a favorable environment for the ordering of the National System of Science Technology and Innovation (SNCTeI), through the establishment of guidelines and incentives for specialization and search for excellence among the actors that make it up.	It provides fundamental theoretical elements, a diagnosis and set of processes to be able to determine the functioning of the system, recognizing its shortcomings and strengths.
Green Book.	The Green Book 2030 that Colciencias presents to the country is a first step for the renewal of the national science and innovation policy, developing its strategic level by defining a conceptual basis, principles and routes for public action, as well as interactions between diverse actors of the National System of Science, Technology and Innovation (SNCTeI).	This text, which was adopted as a guideline for innovation and research for the year 2030, was adopted on July 9, 2018 and presents a retrospective analysis of the policy of innovation in Colombia, highlighting objectives, principles and guidelines of the policy with a focus transformative in science and innovation.

Table 5 Key documents for the construction of innovation policy. Source: Own construction on COLCIENCIAS (2018)

Although, the foundation of the documents is well intentioned and provides tools to insert innovative strategies and procedures in the productive sectors, even with the reduction of taxes for those companies and productive units that generate these processes, the reality of the investment in the sectors it is different, in as much, a harmonization is needed that involves the real sectors of the economy, abandons the academicism and the ostracism that has characterized COLCIENCIAS in the last years, performing functions of control and judge, more than in reality of promoter of innovation policies.

The IDB (2010), for example, suggests that the incentive to create productive units presents a positive correlation with the establishment of policies and a much more stable regulatory framework for innovation policy, which is reflected in state regulations. . According to the same institution:

> In 2009, the average number of procedures required to register a company in OECD countries was in the 6, while in LAC it was around 10. That number has decreased slightly in the region with respect to that registered for 2003. Colombia, Paraguay, Nicaragua and Guatemala have considerably simplified their procedures for the registration of companies. However, in some LAC countries the regulatory burden for the creation of companies remains high. In 2009, 67 days were needed in the region to register a new company, while in the OECD economies an average of 13 days was needed. In Mexico, Panama, Jamaica and Peru, the number of days needed was less than the average for the region. At the opposite end of the spectrum, Haiti, Brazil, and Venezuela needed more than 100 days (195, 120, and 141 days, respectively) (IDB, 2010, page 57)[3].

The reduction in time and requirements is an important step for the entrepreneur at the micro level, to start taking into account the set of resources that could be used for investment in innovation, especially in a context, such as that of the countries of the zone, which is characterized by high levels of informality and little legalization of productive units.

Some Traditional Strategies with the Innovation component.

Although, until now we have found an overview, which illustrates somewhat the current situation of investment in our countries in the field of innovation, it is important to make some observations regarding the way in which, from different aspects of the study of the traditional firm-, contributions can be made that contribute to improve the incorporation of innovation. Internally, the different strategies that small entrepreneurs seek to introduce innovation processes can be defined based on what was proposed by Ortiz (2006):

---

[3] Own translation.

FINANCIAL

Strategic objectives	Effect Indicators	Causal indicators
Increase in income	Percentage of income resulting from the innovations of the process.	Process innovations
Reduction of the cost structure	Costs; income / employees	
Improve the investment process	Investments in HR (Human Resources) / Sales; Investments in innovative processes / Sales.	Availability for investments

CUSTOMERS

Strategic objectives	Effect Indicators	Causal indicators
Increase customer satisfaction	Defects; returns, claims.	Product quality and service.

INTERNAL PROCESSES

Strategic objectives	Effect Indicators	Causal indicators
Improve processes	Process capacity (time and quality indicators)	Process innovation

LEARNING AND GROWTH

Strategic objectives	Effect Indicators	Causal indicators
Increase the innovation capacity of human resources	Labor productivity	Training and education of employees.

Table 6 Innovation Strategies in SMEs. Source: Own construction on the Ortiz data (2006)

The approach is directly related to four fundamental elements in any productive process: the financial area, customers, internal processes and learning as a leading element of growth. For each of them, strategic objectives and two types of indicators are proposed: *effect and causality*. In the financial element, the maximization of benefits is considered as the basic objective of any productive project. The effect indicator can be defined as:

$$BIEFF_1 = [\text{Income resulting from process innovations / Total income}] *100$$

The causal indicator that accompanies the process objectives can be expressed as:

$$BIEFC_1 = [\text{Number of implemented process innovations / Number of planned process innovations}] *100$$

On the other hand, there is a cost reduction that includes two effect indicators:

$CIEFF_1 = [\text{Total costs / Employees}]$

$CIEFF_1 = [\text{Total income / Employees}]$

With respect to the improvement of investment processes, we find two indicators of effect:

$PIEFF_1 = [\text{Investments in human resources / sales}] *100$

$PIEFF_1 = [\text{Innovative process investments / sales}] *100$

In addition, a causal indicator, which refers to the availability for investments:

$PIEFC_1 = [\text{Available from investments with incorporation in innovation / investments required in the short term}] *100$

Regarding the element that relates to customers, we have the following indicators:

$CIEF_1 = [\text{Defects / Total units produced}] *100$

$CIEF_2 = [\text{Returns / Total units produced}] *100$

$CIEF_3 = [\text{Claims / Total units produced}] *100$

For the quality of the product, surveys can be defined with representative samples that use, for example, rating scales (Likert), to analyze the perception of the product, on the one hand and the service on the other. However, for the internal process of inclusion of innovative elements we could define the following indicators:

$CIEC_1 = [\text{Number of products with investment in innovation processes*(Customers satisfied with the product / total of products sold)}]$

In addition, for the case of the product, we can have:

$CIEC_2 = [\text{Number of services with investment in innovation processes*(Customers satisfied with the service / total of services offered)}]$

If we refer now to the internal processes, we can find that the effect indicators refer to two fundamental elements: time and quality. With respect to the first, we can define an indicator that relates productivity in a specific period, in the creation and / or offer of products and services with innovation incorporation:

$PIIE_1$ = [Number of products with investment in innovation processes / Time frame] *100

$PIIE_2$ = [Number of services with investment in innovation processes / Time frame] *100

With respect to quality control, an indicator similar to that of defects can be used in the case of elements related to customers.

$PIEF_1$ = [Defects / Total units produced with investment in innovation]*100

With respect to the incorporation of processes with investment in innovation, we can define a causal indicator such as:

$PIIC_2$ = [Number of processes with incorporation in innovation/ number of total processes of the firm] *100

With respect to learning and growth processes, we can define the following indicator:

ACE_1 = [(Productivity hour / worker in process with innovation) / (Productivity hour / worker in process that does not include investment in innovation)] *100

With respect to the causal indicator, an indicator can be defined as:

ACC_1 = [Number of training for employees in the production of goods or services with the incorporation of investment in innovation / Total number of employee trainings] *100

The following table condenses the total of the indicators, which can represent a high level of utility for companies that wish to start investing in innovation. A weighting is included in the table for each of the indicators:

CATEGORY	KIND	INDEX	RELATIVE IMPORTANCE
FINANCIAL	EFFECT	BIEFF1 = [Income resulting from process innovations / Total income] *100	0,035
		BIEFC1 = [Number of implemented process innovations / Number of planned process innovations] *100	0,035
		CIEFF1 = [Total costs / Employees]	0,035
		CIEFF1 = [Total income / Employees]	0,035
		PIEFF1 = [Investments in human resources / sales] *100	0,035
		PIEFF1 = [Innovative process investments / sales] *100	0,035
	CAUSAL	PIEFC1 = [Available from investments with incorporation in innovation / investments required in the short term] *100	0,04
CUSTOMERS	EFFECT	CIEF1 = [Defects / Total units produced] *100	0,05
		CIEF2 = [Returns / Total units produced] *100	0,05
		CIEF3 = [Claims / Total units produced] *100	0,05
	CAUSAL	CIEC1 = [Number of products with investment in innovation processes*(Customers satisfied with the product / total of products sold)]	0,05
		CIEC2 = [Number of services with investment in innovation processes*(Customers satisfied with the service / total of services offered)]	0,05
INTERNAL PROCESSES	EFFECT	PIIE1= [Number of products with investment in innovation processes / Time frame] *100	0,0625
		PIIE2= [Number of services with investment in innovation processes / Time frame] *100	0,0625
	CAUSAL	PIEF1 = [Defects / Total units produced with investment in innovation]*100	0,0625
		PIIC2 = [Number of processes with incorporation in innovation/ number of total processes of the firm] *100	0,0625
LEARNING AND KNOWLEDGE	EFFECT	ACE_1 = [(Productivity hour / worker in process with innovation) / (Productivity hour / worker in process that does not include investment in innovation)] *100	0,125
	CAUSAL	ACC1 = [Number of training for employees in the production of goods or services with the incorporation of investment in innovation / Total number of employee trainings] *100	0,125

Table 7 Indicators by innovation incorporation process. Source: Own construction on the approaches of Ortiz (2006)

The indicators can constitute an important strategy so that the small and medium productive units can monitor all their actions in relation to the participation of investment in innovation. Its weighting obeys to equitable criteria for each of its categories and types. This contribution cannot be ignored without taking into account the perspective for Latin American countries in relation to investment, aspects related to their level of development (for example, GDP, per capita) and their influence on the generation of exports. With high levels of technology introduction.

It is important to be able to define which are the factors that are related to the type of market in which the productive units operate and that affect the investment destined to innovation. Some works have focused on the size of the company as an indicator of access possibilities for innovation financing. The work of Lichtenberg and Seigal (1991), focused on the importance of the size of the company mainly in the United States and finds a significant relationship between size and innovation; However, we analyze the fact that larger companies have a higher probability, while small companies must allocate their resources to cover needs that we could call priority, from formalization onwards.

Other approaches, such as those of Sanabria and Vélez (2008), consider that in the services sector investment in innovation would be mainly behaving as a Pareto-style distribution, unlike the traditionally studied Gaussian function. For a schematic presentation of the Gaussian distribution and its function, see Nicholson (2007) and Vera (2018). The following chart shows the behavior of a distribution for both cases:

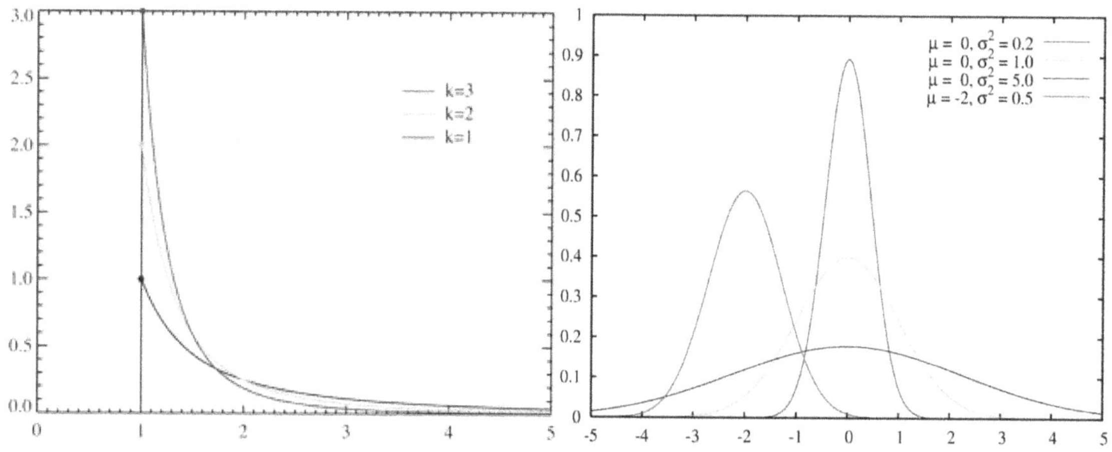

Figure 7Paretian and Gaussian distribution. Source:
https://commons.wikimedia.org/wiki/File:Pareto_distributionPDF.png and
https://commons.wikimedia.org/wiki/File:Normal_distribution_pdf.png

Other studies have focused, for example, on the so-called spillover effect, a concept derived mainly from ecology to refer to the overflow of a certain population that, in the absence of resources, generates an invasion of other habitats, a situation that in the long term contributes to an imbalance of natural systems. Research such as Raut (1995), which finds that investing in innovation for some companies that want to involve elements of research and development, is not relevant the relationship between innovation vs competition. However, this set of findings is not important when analyzing the behavior of the sectors together.

Referencies.

Álvarez, Esteban y García, William (2012). Determinantes de la innovación: Evidencia en el sector manufacturero de Bogotá. En: *Semestre Económico, 15(32), pp. 129-160*

Anderson, Stephen (2017): Llevando Innovaciones en Programas educativos a gran Escala: Perspectivas, estrategias y desafíos pp. 231-248. En: Innovación y calidad en educación en américa latina Santiago cueto (editor). Iniciativa Latinoamericana de Investigación para las Políticas Públicas (ILAIPP). Perú.

Bertanlaffy, Ludwig (1968). General System Theory. George Brazlier. Inc. New York.

Bravo, E. (2012). Globalización, innovación tecnológica y pobreza. Aproximación a las nuevas conceptualizaciones en Latinoamérica. *Espacio abierto*, *21*(3).

BID (2010). Ciencia, Tecnología e Innovación en América Latina y el Caribe: Un compendio estadístico de indicadores. División de Ciencia y Tecnología Sector Social Vicepresidencia de Sectores y Conocimiento.

BID (2010). La necesidad de innovar: un camino hacia el progreso de América Latina y el Caribe. Documento preparado para la cumbre UE-ALC de jefes de Estado y Gobierno. Madrid.

Buchanan, James (1968). The demand and supply of public goods. Chicago. Rand-McNelly.

COLCIENCIAS (2018). Libro Verde 2030. Política nacional de ciencia e innovación para el desarrollo sostenible. Gobierno de Colombia.

COLCIENCIAS (2016). Documento N° 1602. Actores del Sistema Nacional de Ciencia, Tecnología e Innovación. Adoptada mediante Resolución No. 1473 de 2016. Bogotá D.C.

COLCIENCIAS (2015). Documento CONPES 3834. Consejo Nacional de Política Económica y Social República de Colombia DNP (Departamento Nacional de Planeación). Lineamientos de Política para estimular la Inversión Privada en Ciencia, Tecnología e Innovación a través de Deducciones Tributarias.

Crespi, Gustavo, Fernández, Eduardo, & Stein, Ernesto. (2014). ¿Cómo repensar el desarrollo productivo?. BID Biblioteca Felipe Herrera.

Dhrymes, P. (1994). Topics in advanced Econometrics Volume II. Linear and Nonlinear Simultaneous Equations. Springer-Verlag. New York.

Edquist, C. y Johnson, B. (1997). Institutions and organizations in Systems of Innovation. En: Edquist, C. (ed.). Systems of Innovation. Technologies, institutions, and Organizations (pp. 41-63). London and Washington: Pinter.

Informe Global Innovation Index 2018.

Lichtenberg, F. R. y Seigal, D. (1991). "The Impact of R&D Investment on Productivity - New Evidence Using Linked R&D-LRD Data." Economic Inquiry. 29(2) pp. 203-29.

Kline, S y Rosenberg, N. (1986). An overview of Innovation. En: Landau, R y Rosenberg, N. (eds.), The positive sum strategy (pp 275-306). Washington: National Academy Press.

Kruger Corporation (2017). Informe Anual.

Lall, S. (1992). Technological capabilities and industrialization. World development. 20 (2). 165-186.

Malaver y Vargas, M. (2004a). Los procesos de innovación en América Latina: Aportes para su caracterización. Revista Latinoamericana de Administración. Cladea. (33). 5-33.

Manual de Oslo (2006) Guía para la recogida e interpretación de datos sobre innovación. Organización Cooperación y Desarrollo Económico. OCDE.

Nelson, Richard y Winter, Sidney (1982). An evolutionary theory of economic change.

Cambridge, Mass: Harvard University Press, 437p.

Nicholson, W (2007). *Teoría Microeconómica: Principios básicos y ampliaciones.* Novena Edición. Ed. Thomson. México.

Di Maio, Michele (2003). Explaining Technological Change: A Survey. DRUID Academy Winter 2003, PhD Conference, 26 p.

Ortiz, F. (2006). Gestión de innovación tecnológica en PYMES manufactureras. In *Ponencia presentada en I Congreso Iberoamericano de Ciencia, Tecnología, Sociedad e Innovación, México.*

Raut, L. K. (1995). "R&D Spillover and Productivity Growth: Evidence from Indian Private Firms". Journal of development Economics. 48: 1-23.

Sanabria, N y Vélez, J. (2008). Balances de la Competitividad. Bogotá: Economía y Desarrollo. 2. Universidad Autónoma de Colombia.

Schumpeter, Joseph. (1943). La teoría del desarrollo económico. México D.F: Fondo de Cultura Económica.

Vera, Daniel (2018). La Teoría del portafolio: Un estudio empírico. Estudio empírico con base en una cesta de acciones de tres empresas cotizantes en la Bolsa de Valores de Colombia (BVC)." En: España. Ed: EAE ISBN: 978-620-2-11017-4.

CHAPTER 2

CONSTRUCTION OF A MODEL TO IMPROVE TECHNICAL CAPACITY IN MSMEs.

From the family business to the small and medium enterprise

The historical relationship between family and business is undeniable. Since the industrial revolution and even much earlier, the relationship between family and business has tried to be studied. Concepts such as domestic management and its articulation with the atomic element of the assembly of microeconomics that is the company has tried to be analyzed from different positions. When the family transcends the intimate and interior space that involves a set of relationships between members to encompass a system of relationships already in the field of production, we have a new scenario of emergence of small and medium enterprises.

> Quant á la famille, elle est, aprés tout, l'espace natal de cette discipline, désignée d'un nom dont l'etymologie (οικονομία), est encore sensible dans *des dictionnaires économiques* du XVIIIe siécle, largement consacrés á la gestion domestique (Hirsch, 2007, p. 175).

The family space is precedent of the space of production. Hirsch (2007), refers to the internal management of families that are engaged in a particular productive activity and that with the passage of time constitute a new production sphere characterized by a relatively low working capital, a use of labor less, but much more efficient and a fragmentation of the inputs in favor of the profits obtained in the long term. The small family business can be seen as a joint project, of duration, involving several generations, where parents and relatives combine resources and energies and on the other hand, as a house (of commerce, agriculture and industry), which offers the possibility of a relationship space, under the idea of companionship, the functionality and closeness of a group of employees united under the authority of a business leader who usually behaves like a parent. Production then arises in a domestic space that, as will be seen later, is still preserved.

The analysis of the MSMEs has traditionally been done from a disconnected approach to society, emphasizing its internal operational aspects, from a biased view and as Zerda & Rincón (1998) would say far from the real world.

In conventional economics, the treatment of small and medium enterprises has been impregnated with the halo of pseudo precision that marginal analysis gives, enclosing it in the efficiency curves that place it as the paradigm of production in perfect competition, far from the real world of mega and meso-corporations that cohabit with business units of different sizes, rationalities and determinations (Zerda & Rincón, 1998, p.21).

The so-called neoclassical economists elaborate a conception of the market centering their analysis on the absence of predominance or economic powers, under the assumption of perfect competition. Post-Keynesians, emphasizing the criticism of this position, point their criticism to the fact that in the economic structure levels of concentration are observed that generate industrial inequalities. Originally, however, the operational units could not be separated from a direct relationship with traditional craftsmanship, with respect to the participation of the means of production and at the same time with an intensive use of labor power.

In their work, Zerda & Rincón (1998), distinguish three historical stages in the analysis of small and medium industries: adolescence that would be more related to the step of artisanal production to the formalization of productive units, which are gradually leaving On the other hand, labor intensity in favor of capital; a second stage that is mainly related to an emphasis, in some cases even irrational, in the production of employment and in becoming a device for economic development and a final stage that could be defined as a dynamic stage of the economy and based on the emphasis on certain productive factors or technologies and suggest, without being a defined historical stage, a so-called subsistence enterprise that is part of competitiveness issues in a market characterized by excessive cannibalism. The following table shows these different stages of development of small and medium enterprises:

Adolescence	Generation of employment	Dynamizing the Economy
Late-modern dichotomy. Emphasis is placed on the transition from companies that go from artisanal production to small-scale companies. At this moment, the influence of the merchants is preponderant in that the system of advances is generated or what in German is called ***Verlasgssystem***, which indicates a subordination of the artisan to the merchant, who grants raw materials and pays a salary.	This second approach is sustained in Fordism, which is in turn a technique of division of labor and intensification of mass consumption, which generates a cumulative regime. In this perspective, companies could only survive if they increase in size and would be subject to pressures from large companies and corporations.	The fundamental characteristic of this stage of development of the MSMEs refers mainly to the intensive use of hard technology and skilled labor. The investment in technologies is much lower than what the training of skilled labor implies. In other words, the payment of better wages for skilled labor is compensated by a decrease in the cost of acquiring technology because it is very specific (Matamoros, 1989).

Table 8 Stages of development of MSMEs. Source: Own construction on the approaches of Zerda & Rincón (1998)

The subsistence company is that company that survives in an aggressive market logic in which there is a constant struggle to attract consumers, competing with strategies of what has been called savage capitalism. Gómez & Villaveces (1979), consider that this type of company is characterized by simple levels of technology and little or no skilled labor.

> Those who are interested in promoting SMI (small and medium industries) for their "social function", an obligation is imposed on them: to gradually include technologies that are more complex and to qualify the labor force. The emphasis is on technology and the capacity for innovation. In contrast, the promotion of dynamic PMIs is focused on credit. As they do not have assets in which to support the loans, due to the scarce constant capital with which they work, and as the volume of the profit is not constant, due to the movements of demand, the financial system does not easily grant credits. (Zerda & Rincón, 1998, p.37).

As an example, to the little capacity of investment in technology by MSMEs, is the work done by Muñoz et. Al., (2014), about the implementation of improvement strategies in software use procedures, focused mainly on analyzing a set of MSMEs, in the region of Zacatecas (Mexico), dedicated specifically to the creation and development of software, where it was found, for example, that the improvement of software processes generates strategic advantages, which have an impact on the final quality of the products and services offered. The authors' findings suggest, for example, that the majority of SMEs interviewed and developing software have not implemented standardized models that improve their development processes, with a lack of definition of roles with respect to the implementation of such models. The study analyzes organizational elements, financial resources, human resources, processes, projects and finally models and standards. It is likely that the situation is worst in many other Latin American countries, a situation that is generated mainly by deficiency in access to credit for the financing of soft and / or hard technology.

Financing and access to credit

This element is still preventing substantial improvements in the country's productivity. As Botello (2015) argues, the presence of financing problems can have a negative impact on the functioning of MSMEs, which are characterized above all by a low level of capital generating difficulties in self-financing. If we follow the historical line that states that MSMEs are a development device, weaknesses in their internal organization and access problems to credits, they can generate negative consequences in their survival:

> This situation poses structural weaknesses at the macroeconomic level if the importance of SMEs in Latin American economies is taken into account, in Colombia, close to 67% of employment and 40% of production is generated from this type of companies. It is also worth noting that nearly 40% of SMEs are

informal, which restricts their access to formal credit markets even more (Botello, 2015, p, 138)[4].

The table shows the importance of SMEs in the generation of employment and production in several Latin American countries and their comparison with Europe:

Countries and Europe	% Contribution to employment	% Contribution to GDP
Argentina	70,2	53,7
Brazil	59,8	34,3
Chile	63	20,4
Colombia	67,2	38,7
Ecuador	55	20
Mexico	75	62
Paraguay	77	-
Peru	67,9	55,5
Uruguay	68,5	-
Venezuela	38,1	50,2
Europe	67,1	57,6

Table 9 Importance of MSMEs in production and employment. Source: Arazi y Baralla (2012)

In the case of Colombia, it is observed that it beats Brazil and Venezuela in generating employment; in contribution to GDP only exceeds Chile and Ecuador. These data can offer a negative perspective in relation to the incidence of these in the Colombian vs. Latin American context or of their deepening in economic development. In spite of the economic stagnation of the region and the crises experienced by countries such as Argentina, Uruguay and Brazil, the demands of multilateral organizations such as the IMF and the World Bank have not been relaxed:

> These agencies continue to firmly seek, by all means, to raise the level of transferable surplus, either through payment of interest, dividends and profits, or through greater openness to the exploitation of natural and energy resources by large foreign corporations and the international financial organisms, or with the deregulation of the local economy, for the increasing penetration in the most profitable sectors of said corporations (Correa & Girón, 2006, p, 15)[5].

Most of the countries of the region have sought as a strategy for development the increase of direct foreign investment and capital account, as well as in the incentive to internal entrepreneurship or the creation and strengthening of small and medium enterprises, but

---

[4] Own translation.
[5] Own translation.

this it has not been accompanied by significant increases in access to credit, since the interest charged in relation to the total loans is still disproportionate.

For Valadez, Palma, & Cordova (2016), financing must be understood as the set of mechanisms by means of which, a company obtains resources that allow it to achieve objectives in various projects and that are generally used to obtain intermediate goods and payment of other commitments. For many MSMEs, financing is an element of economic stability. The authors distinguish two forms of financing:

a. Internal: that arises from the financial self-sustainability of the productive unit.

b. External: which is the most common and which is expressed in the growth of the company's capital stock, including the injection of capital by new members or with credits obtained from different sources of financing.

A significant number of MSMEs are under the obligation that their needs in terms of liquidity be tied to obtaining microloans through external indebtedness. One of the elements that insist Valadez, et al., (2016), is the need to generate better levels of decision in MSMEs, with respect to the type of financing chosen, making their choices are rational and therefore sustainable in the weather. This is achieved through an adequate dissemination of information regarding the different mechanisms and channels of access to credit.

Access to credit for Colombia is made through commercial banks, commercial financing companies and cooperatives that make up the Colombian financial system. Five of the twenty-one banks in the country have specialized in the supply of credit for the micro, small and medium-sized enterprises sector, as expressed by Zuleta (2011). Another possibility is access to credit through a private financial entity, using BANCOLDEX, a bank for business development and foreign trade in Colombia as an intermediary. Another intermediary is the National Guarantee Fund (FNG). Despite this, the increase in microcredit in recent years has not been significant. The percentage of increase in microcredits is shown in the following graph. These indicate that of the total general credit (which includes consumption, commerce, and housing), this only represents 2% for the years 2005, 2006, 2007, 2008 and 2010. In the time series 2004 to 2013, access to microcredit has grown in its share in the last three years of the series only by 1%

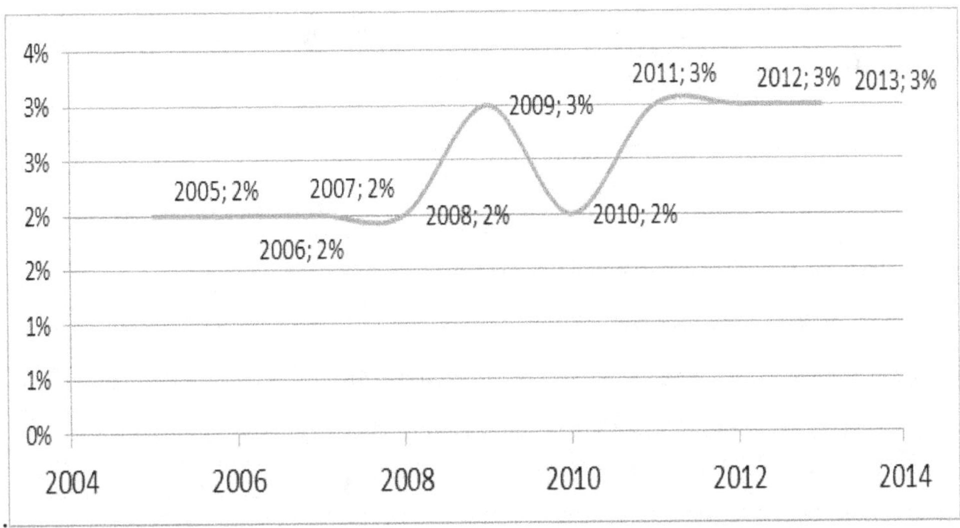

Figure 8 Percentage of Microcredit on total credit 2004-2013. Source: Own construction on the data of the Bank of the Republic.

For Botello (2015), the interest rates for access to microcredit are closer to those of consumption, but much higher (19-32%), compared to the types of commercial and housing interests found in a range (3-17%), so the elements that affect the financing of small businesses are: i) size of the company; ii) age of the signature; iii) internal characteristics, iv) technological capabilities and v) sector and location differences[67].

In addition to the problem of lack of access to credit, we also find informality in the functioning of many MSMEs. Sánchez (2013), considers that the idea of informality has been installed in the Latin American debate, mainly due to the urbanization that the zone has had and the most difficult, due to the consolidation of the national production processes, the migration from the countryside to the city and the growing expansion of large cities, which are parallel processes that hinder the creation of productive units in the rural sector. The problem has been studied from different approaches: structuralism, (neo) institutionalism, neoliberalism, and has been referred, also, by different institutions such as the PREALC (Regional Employment Program for Latin America), the ILO (International Organization for work) and the World Bank. The following graph shows the situation of

---

[6] Other analyzes, such as in the case of García & Dueñas (2016), emphasize the need to begin a solid relationship between MSMEs and the new accounting information standards through the International Financial Reporting Standards IFRS. This, as is obvious, implies for MSMEs, administrative costs, which must be taken into account simultaneously with the fact of the dynamic and changing nature of IFRS, which implies a constant process of updating, for which in many cases the productive units are not ready.

[7] Own translation.

informality for the Colombian case measured for the period of the years 2008-2012, carried out by the DANE, based on companies of 10 workers[8]:

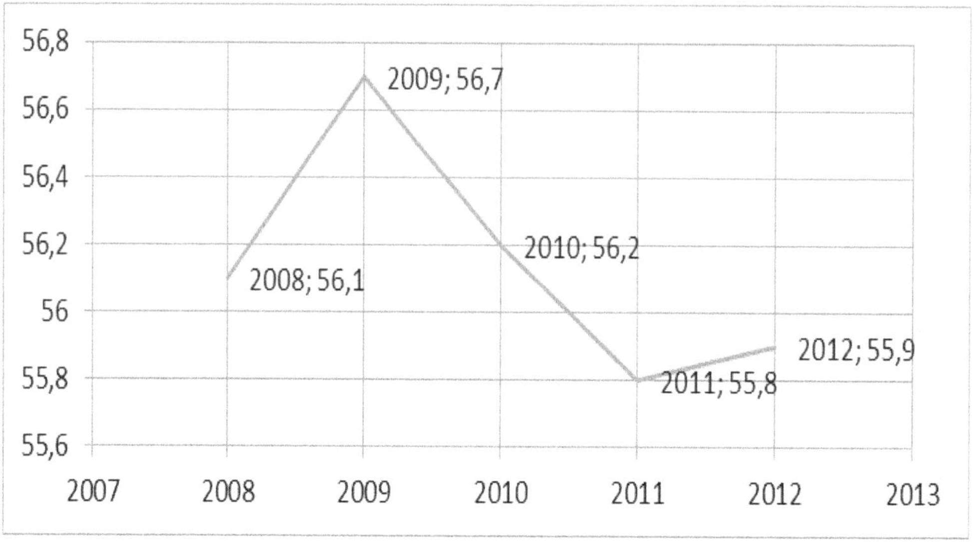

Figure 9 Levels of Informality 2008-2012 in Colombia. Source: Own construction based on data from DANE 2009.

These levels of informality are close to percentages higher than 50%, a situation considered critical since this means that more than half of the economically active population is in a situation of informality.

Production, capacity, and costs

However, perhaps the most significant element has to do with the improvements in the technical capacity of MSMEs and that can be analyzed through a model that involves the recognition of operating costs, acquisition costs per unit of capacity and investment that effectively depends on access to credit. According to Deslandes (1975), to measure the capacity of competition, the manufacturing costs must be considered, at different levels of capacity. This implies the calculation of the main costs: raw materials and materials, labor, maintenance, and manufacturing expenses in general that would include items such as energy, fuel, among others. The manufacturing cost must be compared with the production capacity and the investment. This relationship is defined as the technical critical mass, which ignores elements such as administrative expenses and the fact that the MSMEs does

---

[8] It is important to recognize that since 2009, the DANE reduced for the measurement of informality, the establishments of the sample of 10 employees to five employees. See: National Administrative Department of Statistics (DANE) (2009a). "Methodology informality. Great Integrated Household Survey ". Directorate of Methodology and Statistical Production, National Administrative Department of Statistics, Available at: http://www.dane.gov.co/files/investigaciones/boletines/ech/ech_informalidad/metodologia_ informality.pdf (June 26, 2012).

not produce at full capacity (criterion of technical inefficiency). This relationship, that is, the *critical technical mass*, is usually expressed as follows:

$$\frac{P2}{P1} = \left[\frac{C2}{C1}\right]^{-a}$$

(1)

This relationship between P, which corresponds to the unit cost of operation and the capacity of production unit C, taking into account the number of units performed per unit of time, involves a factor called volume factor a, which is negative expressing a relationship Inverse between operating unit cost and capacity. If another variable is related such as the cost in equipment per unit of capacity (Q), with the increasing capacity of the productive unit, we have the following expression:

$$\frac{Q2}{Q1} = \left[\frac{C2}{C1}\right]^{-b}$$

(2)

In this case, b corresponds to the volume factor. If we finally relate investment I with technical capacity C, we find an expression similar to the previous ones, but unlike the previous ones, the coefficient f is positive, which corresponds to the volume value and which is in this case the value of a positive slope.

$$\frac{I2}{I1} = \left[\frac{C2}{C1}\right]^{f}$$

(3)

It is up to the small producer or manager of the MSMEs, to achieve returns to scale for long-term growth, reducing unit costs and equipment costs per unit of capacity, but increasing the amount of investment. The technical capacity of our small companies can be broken down into different aspects that incorporate improvements in production processes. In the study carried out by Barriga (2006), where 466 small and medium-sized companies were analyzed, variables such as innovation, learning (internal training), access to financial resources and management of finances, influence of management were used as analytical factors. Alternatively, management style and production levels, which make up a complex ICC indicator, which is expressed in the following results:

Score	Innovation	Learning	Finance	Management	Marketing	Production	Average ICC
Very low	25,10	19,50	2,40	3,20	1,70	8,60	5,80
Low	35,60	28,30	10,90	17,60	7,30	42,50	23,20
Middle	24,50	34,50	22,70	31,10	30,70	37,10	36,10
Middle-High	10,70	13,30	36,50	30,70	27,00	10,90	27,00
High	4,10	4,30	27,50	17,00	33,30	0,90	7,90
Total	100,00	100,00	100,00	100,00	100,00	100,00	100,00

Table 10 Small and Medium Enterprise Complex Indicator. Source: Barriga (2001). Based on Hernández y Mendoza (2008)

If we analyze these results, we find that the general average of the complex index studied by Barriga (2006), considers that the status of small and medium-sized companies surveyed is at an average level compared to the adoption of most factors and it is significant to find low levels of incorporation in areas such as innovation and learning. On the other hand, the best scores are in incorporation of procedures for a better management in financial and marketing aspects. This supposes to think that the small and medium company could be focusing its interests on factors related to advertising to increase its demand and in the proper management of the financial resource. However, relatively low values are found in aspects such as production with a low level of 42.5, which indicates a low incidence in the improvement of production through the incorporation of equipment and reduction of production costs.

The concern for the financial aspect could be related to the incorporation of higher credit levels, but which are limited to the demands of the current enterprise. On the other hand, another element that can be a basic factor for MSMEs, in their economic development and their particular interest in generating surpluses, has to do with the use of tools that allow them to define production objectives, based on costs and the use of factors such as labor and capital. Classical theories about production have emphasized, for example, the concept of production function and cost function.

$$x = Aa^{\alpha}b^{\beta}$$

(4)

Where x refers to production, a is the labor force, b is capital. On the other hand, and β, it refers to the elasticities of labor and capital. The function has the property of being a homogeneous function in the following degree: if the sum of both elasticities is 1, then the function is linear and implies a constant increase in returns to scale; in the case where y β <1 or that and β> 1, indicates an increase and decrease, respectively, in returns to scale. The so-called marginal rate of substitution can be expressed as:

$$MRS = \alpha b / \beta a$$

(5)

However, at the same time that they have been studied at the same time, production functions different from the Cobb-Douglas production function and from statistical considerations, in many cases the results have not been satisfactory with respect to the form of the production function, especially when time series analyzes have been done. The research that has been based on cross-sectional data does not offer a satisfactory set of explanations regarding dynamic aspects of the production of companies and especially small businesses[9].

One way of estimating possible economic growth can be done through the reformulation that can be made of this function, using natural logarithms. Since the coefficients $\alpha + \beta = 1$ are homogeneous and there are constant returns to scale, the function can be expressed as follows, as a percentage variation of production in terms of capital and labor factors:

$$\%\Delta Y \cong (\%\Delta A) + \alpha(\%\Delta K) + (1 - \alpha)(\%\Delta L) \tag{6}$$

Where:

$\%\Delta Y$ = Expected GDP variation rate
$\%\Delta TFP$ = Growth Total factor productivity.
$\%\Delta K$ = Growth Stock capital
$\%\Delta L$ = Growth in the number of employees
α = Elasticity of capital over production

Generally, this production function is accompanied by a cost restriction that is expressed through an isocost function, which expresses the relationship between financial capital or productive investment, the payment of the labor factor per unit of time and the cost of use of capital that includes depreciation plus interest. The formalization of an isocost function is expressed as follows[10]:

$$C = w\mathrm{L} + r\mathrm{K} \tag{7}$$

Where:

C = Financial capital
L = Work factor
K = Capital factor
r = Cost of capital use
w = salary

The formalization of the model can finally be expressed through the following equations:

---

[9] For a formalization of the Cobb-Douglas function see León, P. (1967). Structural Change and Growth in Capitalism. The John Hopkins Press. Baltimore, pp, 5-6.

[10] Sánchez, M. (2013). Solved exercises of intermediate Microeconomics. University of La Salle. Faculty of economics and social sciences. Bogotá, p, 8.

$$Max(k,l) = A a^{\alpha} b^{\beta} \tag{8}$$

Subject to:

$$C = wL + rK$$

The explanatory model that emerges from the theoretical explanations, from the interaction of the capacity of the productive unit with the investment, the costs in equipment per unit of production and the unit cost of operation and finally the production function, implies the use of productive factors such as labor and capital, subject to a budgetary restriction of these factors that is expressed through an isocost function. This theoretical corpus can allow small and medium enterprises to be able to have better performance and be able to advance in their articulation with an increasingly competitive market.

Cost analysis is another fundamental element that small and medium enterprises must take into account in order to establish mechanisms that are in accordance with the quantity of goods and services produced and that in the long term allow obtaining significant returns that allow access to the meso production system. Generally, costs have been classified as fixed and variable costs, and are values by means of which a cost function can be established, which should not be confused with the mathematical expression of isocost, because they do not represent the same relation. The cost function establishes a causal relationship between quantities produced and total costs, while the isocost formula, relates costs with two productive factors namely: capital and labor. In general, terms, we can consider the costs of a company as the set of the obligations in money that it incurs to generate certain levels of production. According to Leftwich (1972), everything that the company has to pay for the resources it will use generates a cost outlay (The cost function is a very important mathematical tool that allows the producer to make projections based on the costs you incur or incur in. Generally, a cost function can be expressed as:

$$C = FC + UVC*Q \tag{9}$$

Where:

C = Total Costs

FC=Fixed costs

UVC = Unitary or average variable costs

Q = Production level

This cost function has the structure of a linear function in which the costs are a function of the quantities produced, the slope of the function corresponds to the average variable or unit costs of production and the cut-off point with the y-axis corresponds to the fixed costs. The slope is positive as costs increase according to the production and especially in productive units that have not reached returns to scale or economies of scale. Some costs are independent of the level of production of the company, the fixed costs, while other costs vary according to the level of production. Varian's (1996) presentation of the cost function can be expressed as follows:

$$c(y) = c_v\,(y) + F \tag{10}$$

Where F, is the fixed cost, the average variable cost, and the level of production. In addition, it distinguishes between the average cost function, which measures the cost per unit of production; *the average variable cost function, which measures the variable costs for each unit produced and the average fixed cost function*, which takes into account the fixed costs per production unit. From there, the following equation is derived:

$$CMe(y) = \frac{c(y)}{y} = \frac{c_v(y)}{y} + \frac{F}{y} = CVMe(y) + CFMe(y) \tag{11}$$

In the following graph, we find the relationship between variable, fixed and total costs:

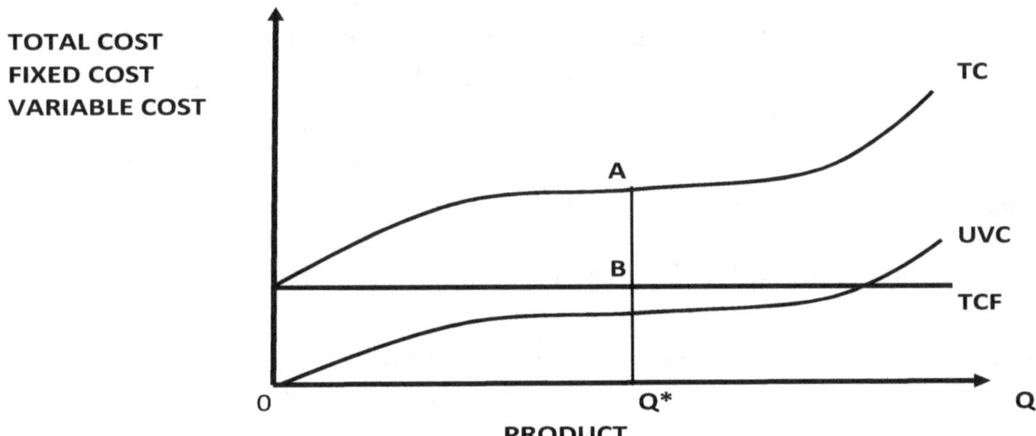

Figure 10 Relationship between total, fixed and variable costs. Source: Own construction on the theory of costs.

If the previous graph is analyzed, it can be found that the total fixed cost TFC remains constant at any level of production; the classical example is expressed through the capital goods whose value remains fixed for any level of production Q. On the other hand, total variable costs increase simultaneously with production. The sum of both costs allows obtaining the total cost. The curves of Total Cost TC and Variable Cost VC have an analogous behavior and their slopes with similar. The fundamental difference would be given by the fixed cost AB for a production level, in this case Q *. The following table allows to understanding the key elements to be considered by the small and medium producer, for the analysis of the production and the factors involved in it:

Unit Cost of production vs Production capacity	Cost in equipment per unit of capacity vs Production	Investment vs Production capacity	Cobb-Douglas Production Function and marginal substitution rate	Cost function and Isocost
$\dfrac{P2}{P1} = \left[\dfrac{C2}{C1}\right]^{-\alpha}$	$\dfrac{Q2}{Q1} = \left[\dfrac{C2}{C1}\right]^{-b}$	$\dfrac{I2}{I1} = \left[\dfrac{C2}{C1}\right]^{f}$	$x = Aa^{\alpha} b^{\beta}$ $MRS = \alpha b/\beta a$	$C = FC + UVC*Q$ $C = wL + rK$

Table 11 Summary equations. Source: Own construction on the approaches of León (1967), Deslandes (1975) and Sánchez (2013)

On the other hand, elements more related to physical aspects of the MSMEs can be analyzed. In a study conducted by Londoño & Navas (2008) about the migration of buyers from the supermarket to the neighborhood store in the city of Cartagena, where it was evident that from MSMEs dedicated mainly to commercial activities, it is considered important or relevant to take into account the following aspects: sales method (counter, self-service or the use of both strategies, number of references sold by the MSMEs, forms of payment offered by the establishment, area of the establishment in square meters, establishment schedule; Income from sales and finally the profit margin These elements, although they are only referred to the analysis through the cluster, should be taken into account as basic elements in the perspective of the MSMEs in its evolution, since these factors have a direct impact in daily operation.

Exogenous elements that affect MSMEs in Colombia

According to data provided by the Spectator on February 18, 2009, 89% of micro, small and medium-sized companies of family origin are not aware of the importance of ensuring the follow-up of the same through the formation of a new leader, or what Hirsch (2007), recognized in the historical course, as the relationship between leader and fatherhood in the family business. FUNDES (Monsignor Abraham Escudero Montoya Foundation for Higher Studies), conducted a study in Bogotá in 2007 with the support of Banco de Bogotá, where it shows aspects related to the uncertainty regarding the financing after the liquidation of the company and, On the other hand, in the perception that the delegation of intra-generational functions constitutes a risk. The failure of them is mainly due to conflicts between family members, as well as the retirement or the risk of disappearance of the founding people and the mechanism of profit sharing.

Regarding the concentration of the same, for the same year 2009, it is found that most of them are concentrated in the city of Bogotá with 63%, followed by the city of Medellin with 13%. Other important cities are Cali, Barranquilla, and Bucaramanga. Figure 7.5 shows the concentration for these cities:

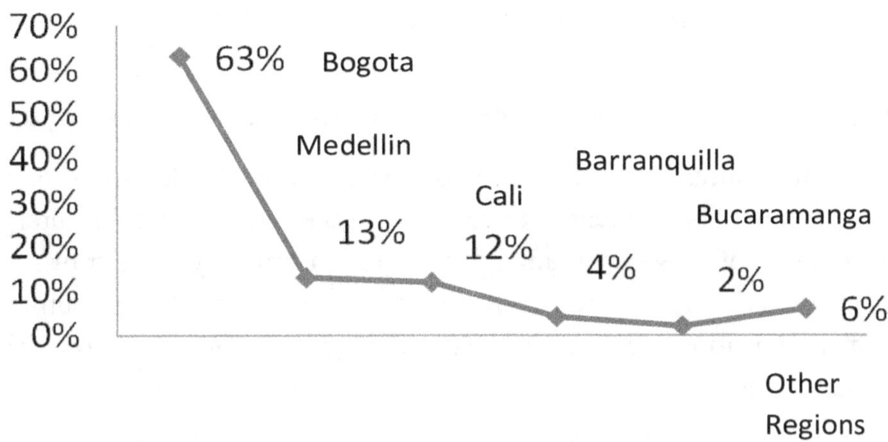

Figure 11 Percentage of MSMEs by City 2009. Source. Own construction.

The high concentration of MSMEs in the nation's capital implies the generation of strategies from different sectors in their strengthening and assumes a significant increase in the treasury and new opportunities for local development for the city. Some deficiencies regarding the internal organization of MSMEs can be evidenced by the fact that 49% have not yet managed to establish conditions for the retirement of members, 45% have not managed to establish a distribution of capital, nor the existence of protocols for the solution of possible conflicts. According to the same study of 2009, family businesses represent 70% of the total number of companies in the country.

For the specific case of the Colombian context, MSMEs is a company created from an innovative idea, which encourages employment, contributes to economic development, and satisfies the need of some economic sector. According to Law 590 of 2000 and its modification, in Law 905 of 2004, small and medium enterprises are entities of economic exploitation that can be executed by a natural or legal person in activities: agricultural, industrial, commercial or rural services or urban The requirements that are established for its categorization are those found in next table:

SIZE	NUMBER OF EMPLOYEES	TOTAL ASSETS
Medium Company.	Between fifty-one (51) and two hundred (200) workers	Between five thousand one (5,001) and thirty thousand (30,000) SMMLV (current legal monthly minimum)
Small Company.	Between eleven (11) and fifty (50) workers	By value between five hundred one (501) and less than five thousand (5,000) SMMLV
Microenterprise.	No more than ten (10) workers	Excluded housing value less than five hundred (500) SMMLV

Table 12 Requirements for MSMEs. Source: Information taken from Law 905 of 2004 Art. 02 Definitions

If you add to the facts already mentioned, under access to credit, low representation of the sector within GDP and employment with respect to other countries, high interest rates and the high concentration of these in urbanized areas, the informality of your organization , the scarce information that the entrepreneur has regarding investment opportunities or topics, the absence of organizational charts, internal planning and control, laboratories, research and development departments, together with the lack of training programs for his employees, the precarious use of technology, lack of planning and inadequate use of resources among others, initiatives that promote the implementation of these elements are necessary and therefore the construction of a support model for formalization and support.

Compared to a large industry, where processes are standardized, that is to say, that processes and procedures use high levels of technology, there is already an opportunity for employees to be trained to provide knowledge that allows them to present innovative ideas, in MSMEs; it makes the incorporation of these processes necessary.

According to the annual DANE Manufacturing Survey from 1974 to 1991, which allows analyzing the evolution of working capital and product capital, the companies that implemented a degree of dynamic modernization were the large industries, while the companies that implemented a degree of Lagging modernization has historically been MSMEs. However, in what has to do with labor productivity, it is found that MSMEs have a greater value in terms of being scenarios that foster dynamic development by offering a high amount of relatively well-paid jobs. On the other hand, it becomes important for MSMEs, to enter effectively in processes such as the internationalization of the economy.

For Filion et al., (2011), MSMEs, they must insist on initiatives that allow them to transcend national markets from a model based on local sales, to one that would have the importance of promoting direct exports. Table 13 shows the set of procedures or phases that MSMEs must follow, to reach important levels of internationalization:

Domestic sales	It is characterized by selling products and services in the local market and is completely unaware of the international market.
Indirect export	The MSMEs generates, through market studies, research in the international market and goes to a local or foreign intermediary to guarantee entry abroad. This intermediary can be a commissioned agent, an international business company broker among others, on the other hand, the remuneration is by commission and the main objective is to find new clients with the name of MSMEs.
Direct export	MSMEs advance from the intermediary to their own knowledge of the international market, initiating direct exports, without the need to resort to intermediaries, since their administrative organization and the set of contacts obtained allow them to generate an export flow in the foreign market.

Table 13 Phases or procedures for Internationalization. Source: Own construction based on the proposals of Filión et al., (2011)

Concept of Model

A model in its simplest sense can be defined as the symbolic representation of the design or of a plan (Ackoff, 1961, p.5). You can approach different ways depending on the subject you are referring to. Following Mosterin (s.f), a model seeks to make a scientific analysis of a systems theory. That is, a set of statements, equations, formulas, diagrams, etc., that adequately describe the current functioning of the system, as well as explain what happened in the past and predict what will happen in that system in the future (Mosterin , sf, p. 134). It may happen that systems theories do not find applicable real models.

> Thus, perhaps certain economic theories will only be applicable (they would only have as models) economic systems where competition, transparency and elasticity of certain factors were perfect. While there is no economy of these characteristics, these theories will lack real models (although if they are consistent, they will have numerical models, but that does not interest economists) (Mosterín, s.f., p.135)[11].

Models can therefore be analyzed from a subjective perspective, from a subjective point of view, as a reliable copy of reality with the objective of studying it or as an abstraction, which from some cardinal points can serve as an interpretation for reality or implementation of its basic elements to achieve an objective. In this sense, a model is not only explanatory but seeks to be able to settle through probabilities of success in the real world. The models, as abstractions, move in the space of the probability of their implementation that will depend above all on their approach to reality. As Carvajal (2002) states, the concept of a model is polysemy, but its main conception is that of an object that

---

[11] Own translation.

reproduces itself by imitating it, in this sense it could be associated with the pattern. On the other hand, it can be associated with the notion of ideal perfection, which brings us closer to the epistemological notion of the model concept. From this perspective a model can be:

i)   An idealization, in that it provides a sample of a system or phenomenon in perfect conditions.

ii) A schematic approximation of some inflection points or significant variables, bearing in mind that reality is unfathomable and difficult to grasp.

These typical model definitions can, in turn, be related to the definition of model types. For Carvajal (2002), the types of model can be analyzed from different positions: iconic, analog, topological, symbolic, and mathematical. The characteristics of each of them can be seen in the following table:

Model classes	Features	Example
Iconic	It refers to the property or a set of properties of an event, a system, a process and can be partially (scaled) or physically represented in a partial way.	Models, flat drawings, scale representations.
Analogue	They are of a much higher abstraction degree than the previous one and are built from analogies based on the qualities of the object to be studied, its structure and the phenomenon or procedure to be studied. They are generally expressed linguistically.	An example is the planetary model as an analogy of the atomic model, the process of ontogenesis and phylogenetic.
Topological	It obeys to the space-time location of elements that are related to each other and that are integrated from resource flows that cross their structure.	Diagrams, tables, diagrams, concept maps, etc.
Symbolic	In this case, the objective elements are represented from equations that do not necessarily present isomorphisms with the structure of the real element. The model is built from these symbols.	The H_2O, as a representation of water.
Mathematical	They are a set of mathematical propositions to express the functioning, theorization, and behavior of a series of variables that make up a model. Their internal relationship allows postulating theorems, assumptions, and postulates.	An equation or an algorithm.

Table 14 Model types. Source: Own construction based on Carvajal's (2002) proposals

With attention to this series of proposals about the notion of a model, it should be borne in mind that a model should not stray from the genuine intention of trying to explain a reality by observing it. In this sense, the business environment, which occurs within an economic structure, is suitable to be analyzed from a model perspective that allows continuous replication in similar contexts and reaches the pattern perspective. The structure of MSMEs, as a set of elements that execute a set of actions from an economic context in which it operates, can be studied from different perspectives that obey an integration of iconic, analog, topological, symbolic and mathematical elements. This structure allows the following elements to be analyzed in small and medium-sized companies: importance of geographic location at scale in a competitive economic and business context; analysis of small and medium-sized companies, using as metaphor their similarity with a living organism; the internal organization of the company from the administrative-organizational point of view; the analysis of cultural elements that cross small and medium-sized companies such as: organizational climate, organizational culture, values, deontological principles, which constitute their own brands and represent permanent symbols of it and finally the establishment of variables that can be related to mathematical models that allow analyzing the development of MSMEs.

United Models

Some elements that are previously exposed are the expression through the model categories proposed by Carvajal (2002), of a model that in turn integrates a set of subcategories and that can be seen in the following table:

Learning	Features	Innovation
Iconic Elements	Model, geographical location in key areas according to the market study	**Domestic Sales**
	Slogan	
	Marketing/Symbol/Brand/Remembering	
Analogical Elements	Birth/Launch/Foundation	
	Competitive growth	
	Decline	
	Relaunch and/or end of MSMEs	
Topological Elements	Organization charts	**Indirect export**
	Division areas	
	Process manuals	
Symbolic Elements	Symbol/Brand/Memory of Brand	
	Organizational Culture	
	Values	
	Ethical principles	
	Organizational climate	
Mathematical Elements	Production function	**Direct export**
	Function and cost structure	
	Efficient use of the productive factor of work (L)	
	Efficient use of capital productive factor (K)	
	Relationship between investment and capital (I)	
	Relationship between operating costs and capacity (P)	
	Relationship between equipment and capacity (Q)	

INPUT — OUTPUT

Table 15 Improvement Model MSMEs. Source: Own construction (2017)

The model corresponds to a systematization of the most significant and relevant elements found in the theories about the development of small and medium-sized production units, according to the different types of models that were categorized through Carvajal's (2002) proposal. . The iconic elements are elements of utmost importance for MSMEs, as they provide a perspective regarding aspects such as location, the memory of it in the client or consumer, aspects related to marketing and advertising, which imply a decision regarding to the costs that the small businessman must incur to generate recognition of the product or service offered.

Although one might tend to think that this element is not so significant in MSMEs, it is enough to know that the positive impression generated through these iconic strategies can generate higher returns. In this sense, the model can be specified as a relationship between the level of importance of each item *(p)*, in the category of elements chosen, -each element that makes up the group of iconic *IE (i)* -, and the costs in that is incurred for its development. That is to say:

$$C_{IE} = p_1 * (C_{gu}) + p_2 * (C_s) + p_3 * (C_{marketing\text{-}symbol\text{-}brand\text{-}remembrance})$$

Where:

C_{IE} = Costs in iconic elements

C_{gu} = Costs in geographic ubication

C_s = Costs slogan

$M_{arketing\text{-}symbol\text{-}brand\text{-}remembrance}$ = Costs marketing

p_n = Level of importance given to it by the small and medium enterprise

Regarding the analogical aspects, the entrepreneur must bear in mind that small and medium-sized companies, like all productive units, go through a business cycle that can have periods of expansion-contraction, which in turn must generate, strategies that take into account: relaunches in declining situations or the expansion of products and/or services. In this sense, the model is a relationship between the levels of importance assigned by the employer to each category, in this case AE (i), for each of the analog elements. However, in addition, it is important to recognize that the entrepreneur incurs costs of launching products and / or services initially that must be considered in the model.

$$C_{AE} = p_1 * (C_{cfps}) + p_2 * (C_{cd}) + p_3 * (C_r) + p_4 * (C_l)$$

Where:

C_{IE} = Costs in analogic elements

C_{cfps} = Costs in creation, foundation, products, and services

C_{cd} = Costs competitive development

C_r = Costs relaunching

C_l = Costs liquidation

p_n = Level of importance given to it by the small and medium enterprise

Topological elements are represented by organization charts, area divisions and administrative processes. These elements have a direct influence on small and medium enterprises, since in the face of any situation that alters their operation, whether due to chance or force majeure, the existence of protocols can reduce internal risks. On the other hand, the clear existence of a division by areas and an organizational chart, allows establishing a flow of information through them and a much more efficient exchange of resources. It could be synthesized in these basic elements:

$$C_{TE} = p_1 * (C_{ao}) + p_2 * (C_{pm})$$

Where:

C_{TE} = Costs in topological elements

C_{ao} = division into administrative areas and organization chart

C_{pm} = protocols and manuals

p_n = Level of importance given to it by the small and médium enterprise

In relation to symbolic elements, these are related to organizational culture, values, deontological principles, and organizational climate. These elements contribute significantly to the internal operation of small and medium enterprises and can be expressed as follows:

$$C_{SE} = p_1 * (C_{ocs}) + p_2 * (C_{ep}) + p_3 * (C_{oc})$$

Where:

C_{SE} = Costs in symbolic elements

C_{ocs} = Costs in organizational culture strategies

C_{ep} = Costs in deontological and ethical principles

C_{oc} = Costs in Organizational climate

p_n = Level of importance given to it by the small and medium enterprise

The elements of mathematical order, as already observed, are already represented in the table where they are considered: the function of production, the function and structure of costs, the efficient use of the capital factor, the efficient use of the labor factor, the relationship between investment, operating costs and equipment with production capacity. To see how these elements are integrated, observe appendix B of the mathematical component at the end of the book, which allows the construction of the multifactorial coefficients of capital and labor (see appendix B).

References

Ackoff, R. (1961). The Design of Social Research. Estados Unidos. The University of Chicago Press.

Arazi, M. C., & Baralla, G. (2012). La situación de las PyMEs en América Latina.Inter-American Development Bank (IADB).

Botello, H. (2015). Determinantes del acceso al crédito de los PYMES en Colombia. En. *Ensayos de Economía*. N° 46. Enero – junio 2015. UIS, pp, 135-155.

Blair, R & Kenny, L. (1983). Microeconomía con aplicaciones a la empresa. Ed. Mc Graw Hill. Madrid.

Carvajal, A. (2002). Teorías y Modelos: Formas de representación de la Realidad. En: *Revista Comunicación* 12/01. Instituto Tecnológico de Costa Rica. Cartago Costa Rica. pp 1-14.

Cobb, C.W. & P.H. Douglas (1928) "A Theory of Production", En: *American Economic Review* 18 (supplement): 139-165.

Correa, E & Girón, A (2006). Reforma Financiera en América Latina. CLACSO Libros. Buenos Aires.

Departamento Administrativo Nacional de Estadística (DANE) (2009a). "Metodología informalidad. Gran Encuesta Integrada de Hogares". *Dirección de Metodología y Producción Estadística, Departamento Administrativo Nacional de Estadística*, Disponible en: http://www.dane.gov.co/files/investigaciones/boletines/ech/ech_informalidad/metodologia_informalidad.pdf (junio 26 de 2012).

Deslandes, H. (1975). Las 8 etapas de un estudio de factibilidad. En. *Administración de Empresas* 6 (61).

Londoño, E, & Navas, M. E. (2009). Actitud de los propietarios de Mypimes de comercio hacia la negociación con proveedores: *Un análisis de clúster*. St. Louis: Federal Reserve Bank of St Louis.

Filión, L, Martinez, L & Morelos, J. (2011). Administración de PYMES emprender a dirigir y desarrollar. México: Pearson.

García-Santillán, A., Rangel, A. C., García-Díaz, R., & González-Gómez, S. (2013). Identifying the actions taken by supply companies enrolled to national financials productive chains program (Mexico). En: *Advances in Management and Applied Economics, 3*(6), 193-215

Gómez, H & Villaveces, R. (1979). La pequeña y la mediana industria en el desarrollo colombiano. Ed. La carreta. Medellín.

Hernández, G & Mendoza, L. (2006). Evaluación de la capacidad tecnológica de las PYMES exportadoras del subsector confecciones en Barranquilla en un mercado globalizado. Trabajo degrado para optar el título de Magister en Administración. Universidad Norte.

Hirsch, J. (2007). Famille et enterprise en histoire. En: *Dictionnaire historique de l'economie-droit XVIIIe – XXe siecles. Droit et Societe 17.* L.G.D.J. Paris.

Horngreen, C. (1991). Contabilidad de Costos. Ed. Prentice Hall. New York.

Leftwich, R. (1972). Microeconomía. Editorial Interamericana. México.

León, P. (1967). Structural Change and Growth in Capitalism. The John Hopkins Press. Baltimore.

Ley 590 de 2000.

Ley 905 de 2004.

Londoño, E., & Navas, M. (2008). Migración de los compradores del supermercado a la tienda de barrio de la ciudad de Cartagena. Memorias de la XLIII Asamblea Anual del Consejo Latinoamericano de Escuelas de Administración. Puebla, México: Cladea.

Matamoros, M. (1989). Las empresas colombianas de base tecnológica: perspectivas económicas y restricciones financieras. En. *Memorias Seminario*

Modalidades de Financiación e Inversión para empresas de Base tecnológica. Assel, Bogotá.

Mayumi, K, Giampietro, M & Ramos-Martín, J. (2012). Reconsideration of dimensions and curve fitting practice in view of Georgescu-Roegen´s epistemology in Economics. En: Romanian Journal of Economic Forecasting. N° 4 /2012, pp, 17-35.

Monteros, E. (2005). Manual de Gestión Microempresarial. Ecuador: Universitaria.

Mosterin, J. (s.f.). Sobre el concepto de Modelo. Universidad de Barcelona. Recuperado de: www.Dialnet-SobreElConcepoDeModelo-2045041.pdf

Muñoz, M., Gasca, G., & Valtierra, C. (2014). Caracterizando las necesidades de las pymes para implementar mejoras de procesos software: Una comparativa entre la teoría y la Realidad/Characterizing SME's needs for implementing a software process improvement: A comparative between the reality and the theory. En: *Revista Ibérica De Sistemas e Tecnologias De Informação,* pp, 1-15.

Polimeni, R & Cols. (1989). Contabilidad d Costos. Ed. Mc Graw Hill. Bogotá.

Valadez, G. V., Palma, I. C., & Córdova, Guadalupe, C. (2016). Importancia y participación de las MIPYMES en la economía mexicana. En: *Institut De Socio-Économie Des Entreprises Et Des Organisations (Écully, Rhône). Recherches En Sciences De Gestion,* (114), 45-75.

Redacción Negocios. (2009, Feb 18). Una radiografía de las pymes familiares. *El Espectador.*

Sánchez, M. (2013). Ejercicios resueltos de Microeconomía intermedia. Universidad de la Salle. Facultad de Ciencias Económicas y Sociales. Bogotá.

Sánchez, R. (2013). Enfoques, conceptos y metodologías de medición de la informalidad laboral en Colombia. En: *Lecturas De Economía, 79,* 12.

Varian, H. (1996). Microeconomía Intermedia. Un enfoque Actual. Ed. Antoni Bosch. Cuarta Edición. España.

Zerda, A & Rincón, N. (1998). La pequeña y Mediana Indsutria en al Encrucijada. Facultad de Ciencias Económicas Programa de Maestría en Economía. Santa fé de Bogotá. D.C.

Zuleta, L. (2011). Políticas e instituciones de apoyo a las pymes en Colombia. (Capítulo III). Apoyando a las pymes: Políticas de fomento en América Latina y el Caribe. Ferraro, Carlo (compilador). En: http://www.mipymes.gov.co/

CHAPTER 3

THE APPLICATION OF DETERMINANTS TO THE RELATIONSHIP BETWEEN PRODUCTIVE FACTORS: *UNDERPRODUCTION* AND PRELIMINARIES OF DIRAC

The interest of economists in physics as affirmed by Contreras and Larralde (2013), has focused mainly on the understanding of financial markets. In the eighties, the academic efforts of Wall Street, concentrated on the analysis of market data, generating a massive recruitment of mathematicians and physicists, some of whose works have been subsequently grouped under the name of *Econophysics*[12]. These works have emphasized statistical physics, stochastic systems, and the complex paradigm. Other relationships between both fields of knowledge are related to the use of concepts such as utility, which was introduced by Daniel Bernoulli, trying to describe through it the preferences of people. Another example, the random walk, has been related to the Brownian movement and as a simile of the movement of prices in the market. The nature of the matter has given scope to the investigation of so-called complex systems, in which supposed small disturbances which will generate significant effects on itself, systems that have been used to explain, for example, global crises, the stock market and volatility of prices, recognizing the rational nature of the intervening agents. In this regard:

> [...] the dynamics of economic systems arise from the activity of agents, sometimes many them, whose decisions affect the options and perspectives of other agents, all with more or less heterogeneous incentives and objectives. Systems of this type have the ingredients and exhibit the properties of complex systems, and therefore, the tools of statistical physics, stochastic processes and non-linear dynamics can be very useful for their analysis (Contreras & Larralde, 2013, p. 6).

On other hand, it has been affirmed that all the neo-Keynesian perspective from, for example, Samuelson's presentations, was based on the idea of equating the laws of thermodynamics (especially the second law), to the equilibrium of economic systems. This relationship, however, has not been exempt from criticism. In this respect, Soler raises:

---

[12]This definition has been attributed to Mantegna & Stanley (2000), who consider it as a multidisciplinary area of combination between physics, economics, mathematics, and finance.

[...] have emerged heterodox economic currents that from the various contributions of contemporary physics and the energy theory of physics, has made serious questions to conventional economic theories. Within this nascent paradigm are inscribed economists such as Daly, Georgescu-Roegen, Henderson, Kapp, Mishan, Naredo, Schumacher, among others, who pose a judgment to the mechanisms of the economic system in light of the second law of thermodynamics and propose new elements for the construction of alternative economic systems (Soler, n.d., p. 37).

On the other hand, we cannot ignore the influence of neoclassical economics in the last century, and the fact that it has insisted on introducing into the marginal economic analysis, a singular weight to the productive factors of labor and capital. Undoubtedly, capitalist economies are supported by an excessive concentration of these factors, to the detriment of others such as land, technology, and innovation. From Solow (1961) and Denison (1961), these new aspects have been incorporated into the study of economic dynamics. The productive factors have generated a deep analysis that has introduced models of economic growth, generally expressed in functions of different types. Next, we will find the definition of both unclear factors:

Work, refers to the time a person spends in production, working in automobile factories, cultivating the land, teaching in a school, or baking pizzas. Thousands of occupations and tasks, for all skill levels, are executed by work. It is the most familiar and crucial input of an advanced industrialized economy ... Capital resources integrate the durable goods of an economy and are used to produce other goods. Among the capital goods are machines, roads, computers, hammers, trucks, steel mills, automobiles, washing machines and buildings. As will be discussed later, the accumulation of specialized capital goods is essential for the task of economic development (Samuelson & Nordhaus, 2010, p. 9).

This neo-Keynesian definition is broad and synthetic, perhaps written for general understanding, without delving into issues much more specific to economic discipline, which requires the construction of a theoretical structure that allows us to demonstrate methods that contribute to the measurement of these factors and its influence on production. In this order of ideas, the production functions studied in microeconomics, generate a significant contribution to the understanding of the interrelation between both factors. The most common are: the linear production function, which presents a similarity with the second equation studied in the Dirac preliminaries (1928), the Cobb-Douglas function, the Leontief production function or fixed proportions and the function of production of elasticity of constant substitution (CES), which, as will be seen below, is similar to the first equation of Dirac's preliminaries (1928), with the exception of the total factor of productivity (A) and its exponents.

Capital and Labor.

The relationship between the preliminaries to the Paul Dirac equation (1902-1984) and the proposed productive factors (capital and labor) has not been explored. However, it is of particular interest to deepen the relationship between the problem encountered by the physicist and the possibility of proposing a similarity with some production functions, which is also based on the ingenious resolution found by Dirac (1928), the equations of his preliminaries. This attempt may suggest a new field of research that considers the interdisciplinary openness between economics and physics and especially in the relationship between capital and labor.

In this sense, the following work seeks to relate Dirac's preliminaries (1928), as two equations that express possible production functions, through a numerical example of productivity expressed by the capital and labor factors for a set of eleven countries for the year 1998, information that was obtained from the works of Aten, Heston & Summers (2002), Bernanke & Gürkaynak (2001) and Barro & Lee (2000). In principle there will be a presentation of some of the main production functions studied in microeconomics, followed by an ***underproduction*** analysis between countries, whose data obtained will be found in appendix C.

Then a formalized presentation of Dirac's preliminaries (1928) will be made, under the assumption that the variables expressed in the equations refer to productive factors capital and labor, to finally show a numerical example that reflects how the determinant of the matrix gives solution to the preliminaries of Dirac (1928), can provide important elements to understand the relationship between the two factors of production.

Some production functions.

Next, there will be a general presentation of some of the most studied production functions: Cobb-Douglas function, linear function, the production function of Leontief or fixed proportions and the production function of elasticity of constant substitution (CES).

Cobb-Douglas production function.

Perhaps, one of the most studied growth models is that which considers production as a homogeneous function between capital and labor together with two parameters that represent the elasticities of both factors. This function, which is called the Cobb-Douglas function, has been widely evaluated and has had a great recognition in the theoretical structure from the neoclassical approach, not without certain criticisms[13].

The Cobb-Douglas function is expressed as follows:

$$(1) \quad Q = f(K,L)$$

$$(2) \quad Q = AK^{\alpha}L^{\beta}$$

Production is a function of the productive factors' capital and labor, where:
Q = production.
L = labor force
K = capital.
α = capital's elasticity.
β = elasticity of the work force.
A = total factor of productivity.

According to Varian (1998):

> If the production function has the form $f(x_1, x_2) = Ax_1^a x^b$, we say that it is a Cobb-Douglas production function. It has the same functional form as the Cobb-Douglas preferences ... since the magnitude of the utility function was not important, we assumed that A = 1 and generally that a + b = 1. But the magnitude of the production function is, so we must allow these parameters to adopt arbitrary values. Parameter A measures, approximately, the scale of production, that is, the volume of production that is obtained if it uses one unit of each factor. Parameters a and b measure the response of the quantity produced to the variations of the factors (Varian, 1998, p. 319).

A traditional graph that shows the behavior of the function, we find it below:

---

[13] On the criticisms of the Cobb-Douglas function see Mayumi, Giampietro & Ramos-Martin (2012).

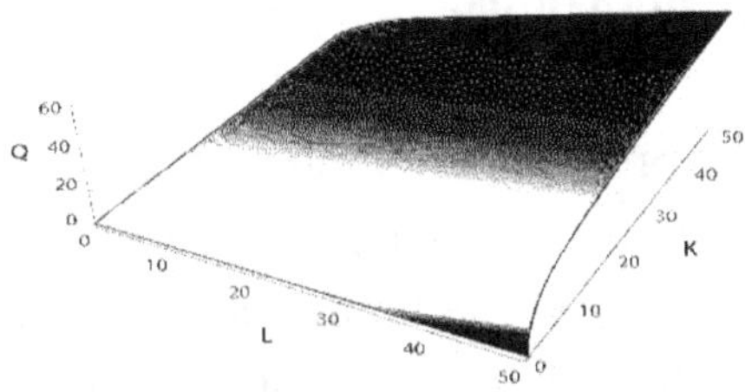

Figure 12 Cobb-Douglas function. Source: http://www.esacademic.com/dic.nsf/eswiki/508355

The homogeneity of the function implies that the sum of the elasticities is equal to 1:

$$(3) \quad \alpha + \beta = 1$$

However, this would be a fundamental economic axiom that has to do with the idea that capital and labor are efficiently used in production, which, from the point of view of the model, is an element that contributes to its robustness, but which empirically assumes that it would not be wasted and both factors would be rationally used. This element of simplification does not correspond to reality and the neoclassical efficiency curves do not contemplate the waste of resources in their analysis. No nation or state will work efficiently, nor use capital adequately, since this would imply ignoring the influence of the elements of uncertainty and risk in the markets.

Linear production function

On the other hand, we have the function of linear production. This is a linear function with two factors that can be expressed as follows:

$$(1) \quad q = f(k, l) = ak + bl$$

For the case of this function, it is considered that it presents constant returns to scale. For t> 1,

$$(2) \quad f(tk, tl) = atk + btl = t(ak + bl) = tf(k, l).$$

The isoquants of this function are parallel lines whose slope is equal to (a-b / a). The technical substitution rate (TTS), for the case of this function, is constant along an isoquant. It is as Nicholson (2007) points out, a very useful function, but little applicable to reality since it assumes that capital and work are perfect substitutes for each other. This means that a company could only use capital and replace everything for work and on the contrary.

Production function of fixed proportions.

The production function of fixed proportions implies that capital and labor must be used in the same proportion and is characterized because the isoquants of the same have the form of an *"L"*. If a productive unit were to execute production based on this function, it will be found that it will operate along a line where the capital to labor ratio K / L is constant. This function can be expressed mathematically as follows:

$$(1) \qquad q = \min(ak, bl) \qquad a, b > 0,$$

The operator *"min"* implies that the production is determined by the lower of the two values between *ak* and *bl*. From this it follows that the use of, for example, a greater amount of labor will not increase production and that for this reason the value of the marginal product will be equal to 0. An example of the application of the production function of fixed proportions is provide in Nicholson (2007):

> For example, many machines require the presence of a certain number of people to operate them, but the excess of workers would be useless. Consider combining capital (a mower) and work to till a field. It will always be necessary for a person to control the mower and one of the factors without the other will not produce anything. It is possible that many machines are of this type and that they require a fixed complement of workers per machine (Nicholson, 2007, p. 197).

A graphic representation of the production function of fixed proportions is the following:

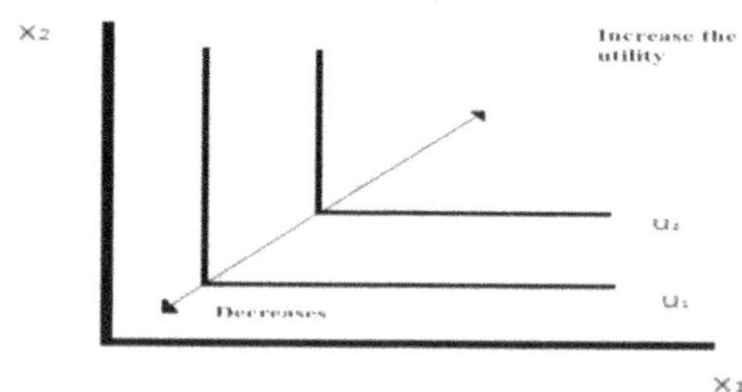

Figure 13 Production function of fixed proportions. Source: Nicholson 2007.

Leontief production function

A special case of production function was enunciated by Leontief. If it is assumed that, a production function has the following presentation:

$$(1) \quad q = f(k,l) = k + l + 2\sqrt{k*l}$$

The function was developed by Wassily Leontief. It exhibits returns to scale:

$$(2) \quad f(tk,tl) = tk + tl + 2t\sqrt{kl} = tf(k,l)$$

With respect to marginal productivities, we can find that these are represented for the case of capital:

$$(3) \quad f_k = 1 + \left(\frac{k}{l}\right)^{-0,5}$$

In addition, for the case of the work factor:

$$(4) \quad f_l = 1 + \left(\frac{k}{l}\right)^{0,5}$$

These marginal productivities have two characteristics. On the one hand, they are positive and on the other hand, they are decreasing. The technical substitution rate depends on the proportion of both factors:

$$(5) \quad TTS = \frac{f_l}{f_k} = \frac{1+\left(\frac{k}{l}\right)^{0,5}}{1+\left(\frac{k}{l}\right)^{-0,5}}$$

On the other hand, the technical substitution rate will present a decrease to the extent that the relationship between capital and labor decreases (k / l). Isoquants have a convex shape. The graphic representation of the Leontief function behaves like a pyramid that reduces its proportion with respect to the productive factors. Below we can find the following:

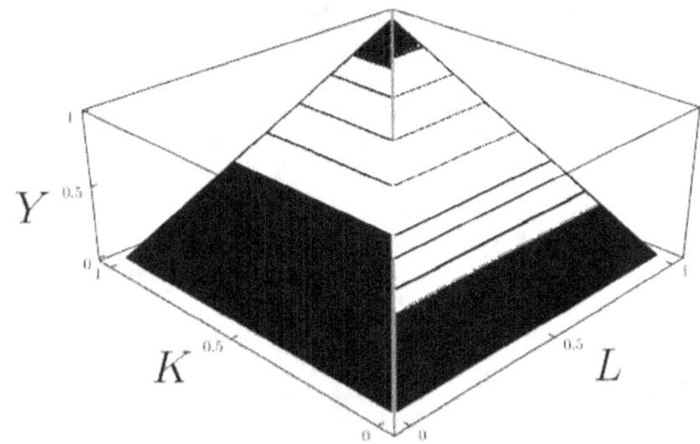

Figure 14 Leontief production function. Source: http: // www. Leontief.png (550 × 354 pixels, file size: 53 KB, MIME type: image / png

CES production function

This function was introduced by Arrow, Chenery, Minhas & Solow (1961) and is determined by the following equation:

$$(1) \quad q = f(k, l) = [k^p + l^p]^{\frac{\gamma}{p}}$$

For the cases in which:

$$(2) \quad p \leq 1, p \neq 0 \ y \ \gamma < 1$$

In the case where $\gamma > 1$, we find that the function has increasing returns to scale and in the opposite case, when it is less than 1 it will have decreasing returns. The technical substitution rate for the case of this function is given by:

$$(3) \quad TTS = \frac{f_l}{f_k} = \frac{\frac{\gamma}{p} * q^{\frac{\gamma-p}{\gamma}} * pl^{p-1}}{\frac{\gamma}{p} ** q^{\frac{\gamma-p}{\gamma}} * pk^{p-1}} = [\frac{l}{k}]^{p-1} = [\frac{k}{l}]^{p-1}$$

When this function is expressed with many factors, we have that it is determined by:

$$(4) \quad q = [\sum \beta_i x_i]^{\frac{e}{p}}, p \leq 1.$$

This function meets the following conditions:
• For each level of production, this function has constant returns to scale whenever e = 1 and in the case where e > 1, it presents increasing returns to scale.
• Marginal productivity is decreasing for each factor p ≤ 1.
• The elasticity of factor substitution (for two factors) is equal to:

$$(5) \quad \sigma = \frac{1}{1 - p}$$

Which is equally admissible when there is substitution between both factors.

Comparisons between countries

If you want to make a comparison of the productivity found between countries, you must divide each of its production functions. So that in equation one (1), the first term of the second member multiplies the quotient between the productivities. As is obvious, if both countries present the same accumulation of factors, the quotient between their levels of production would be equal to the quotient between the levels of factor accumulation. This is the *underproduction* comparison equation:

$$(1) \quad \frac{y_i}{y_j} = \left(\frac{A_i}{A_j}\right) * \left(\frac{K_i^\alpha * h_i^{1-\alpha}}{K_j^\alpha * h_j^{1-\alpha}}\right)$$

This allows measuring the differences in productivity, considering that two of the three terms can be observed directly. This equation fulfills the following conditions, namely:

- The greater the quotient between the different levels of production, the greater the difference in productivity.
- The greater the difference in accumulation between productive factors in both countries, the lower the difference in productivity will be.

Appendix C shows the relative productivities of each country compared to the others, with the United States as reference country. The *underproduction average* shows a privileged position of United States, Japan, Canada, and Finland. The average, however, always should be referenced by countries with respect others (*standard country*).

On other hand, the following equation compares, by a ratio, the productivities of both countries as an equivalent ratio between the production of both countries divided in the use and accumulation of the productive factors. The specific weight of the productive factors in each country will decrease productivity, if relatively stable levels of production are observed.

$$(2) \quad \left(\frac{A_i}{A_j}\right) = \frac{\left(\frac{y_i}{y_j}\right)}{\left(\frac{K_i^\alpha * h_i^{1-\alpha}}{K_j^\alpha * h_j^{1-\alpha}}\right)}$$

Thus, economic growth from a neoclassical perspective has been concentrated in models that have studied the relationship between these productive factors. For example, Lucas (2002), analyzing the model presented by Solow and Denison (1961), on the growth of the United States:

> The main contributions of the neoclassical framework, much more important than its contributions to the clarity of the purely qualitative discussions, arise from its ability to quantify the effects of various growth influences ... the key assumptions are related to the mobility of the factors: can they People and capital move freely? The easiest thing to do is to start with the assumption of no mobility, because then we can treat each country as an isolated system ... In this case, the model predicts

that countries with the same preferences and technology will converge towards identical levels of income and asymptotic rates of growth (Lucas, 2002, pp, 57- 59).

The assumption that productive factors do not move between countries diminishes the versatility of neoclassical models, since the analysis of the productivity of each country would be biased by the unquestionable reality of trade and the possibility of mobility of factors in the post-capitalist economies. In this sense, although the present analysis is based on the appreciation of endogenous productive factors, it does not fail to consider the fundamental fact of the importance of factor mobility. The following table shows the relationship between the uses of productive factors, from different countries with reference to the United States for the year 1998:

Country	Output per worker, y	Physical capital per worker, k	Human Capital per worker, h	Factors of production $K^{1/3}h^{2/3}$	Productivity, A
United States	1,0000	1,0000	1,0000	1,0000	1,0000
Canada	0,7600	1,0200	0,9800	0,9900	0,7700
Japan	0,7400	1,3700	0,8700	1,0000	0,7300
Finland	0,7100	1,1400	0,8900	0,9600	0,7400
United Kingdom	0,7000	0,8000	0,8200	0,8100	0,8700
South Korea	0,4400	0,7500	0,9200	0,8600	0,5100
Mexico	0,3200	0,3600	0,7400	0,5800	0,5500
Peru	0,2000	0,2400	0,7700	0,5200	0,3900
India	0,0860	0,0470	0,5500	0,2400	0,3500
Kenya	0,0410	0,0210	0,5300	0,1800	0,2300
Tanzania	0,0150	0,0190	0,4500	0,1600	0,0940

Table 16 Output, factor of accumulation and productivity in relation to the United States 1998. Source: Own construction on the data of Aten, Heston & Summers (2002), Bernanke & Gürkaynak (2001), Barro & Lee (2000)

The next graphic shows the behavior of the vs he factors (Output per worker, y), (Physical capital per worker, k), (Human Capital per worker, h), Factors of production $K^{1/3}h^{2/3}$[14].

---

[14] $1/3 + 2/3 = 1$. Testing the homogeneity of the function.

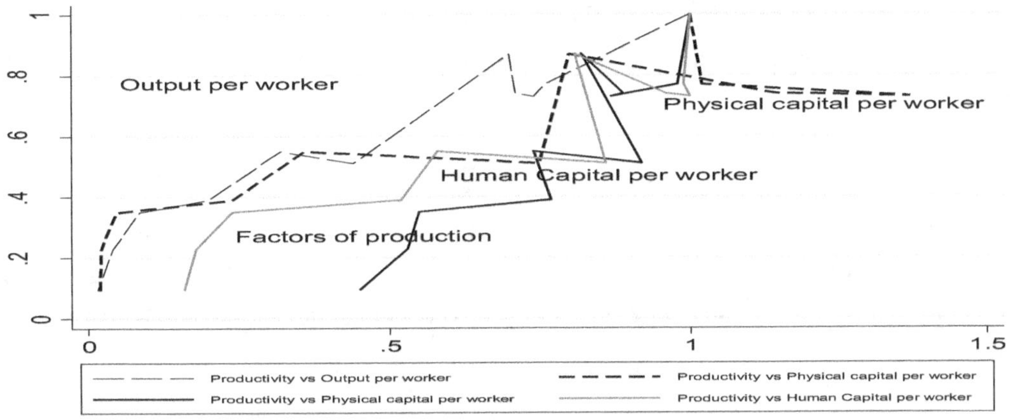

Figure 15 Productivity vs Factors for several countries 1998. Source: Own construction on the data of Aten, Heston & Summers (2002), Bernanke & Gürkaynak (2001), and Barro & Lee (2000).

The relationship provides essential elements for the analysis of the interaction of productive factors. All countries consider it essential to define an approach to the use of capital and labor. In this sense, the Dirac equation that will be explained below can provide an approximate value of the use of the factors.

The preliminaries of Dirac[15].

The path followed by the physicist to solve the equation[16] starts from the following considerations. In principle, Dirac (1928) seeks to find a compatibility between quantum mechanics described in principle by Schrödinger and spatial relativity. Dirac, part of the Schrödinger equation for an electron in an electromagnetic field. The equation is the following:

$$(1) \quad i\hbar \frac{\partial \Psi}{\partial t} = H_\Psi$$

Where:

Ψ = Matter wave equation[17].
i = imaginary unit[18].

---

[15] The presentation of this section is supported by Dirac (1928), Bjorken & Drell (1964), Cottingham & Greenwood (1998) and Mandl & Shaw (1986).

[16] $\sqrt{x^2 + y^2} = ax + by$

[17] De Broglie (1892-1927), had formulated in 1924, the dual character of matter, since, depending on the experiment, it will behave as a corpuscle or as a wave. This variable refers specifically to the wave nature of matter. See. Lawkin, Kerwin (1968).

[18] Imaginary units correspond to complex numbers, which in general terms relate to a real number, multiplied by the imaginary unit, that is, the root of -1. Imaginary unity is vital in quantum physics because it allows simplifying the existence of states of matter in time. Euler and Leibniz have established their use. The first referred to the root of -1, as nonexistent and the second as an intermediate state between being and nothingness.

ħ = Planck constant, divided by 2π or Dirac constant[19].
H = Hamiltonian dependent on time in general, the observable corresponds to the energy of the system[20].
t = time.

In general terms, what Dirac did, was to replace in this equation, the classical variables by the operators, in such a way that taken the relativistic equation for energy, taking into account that the Energy $E \rightarrow i\hbar\partial / \partial t$ $p = -i\hbar \nabla$ In this case p corresponds to the observable impulse:

$$(2) \quad E = \sqrt{m^2 c^4 + c^2 p^2}$$

Where:

c = speed of light.
m = mass.
p = observable impulse.

A first substitution of (2) in (1), would have the following approach. We assimilate H as the energy level of the system. Then H and E are equivalent:

$$(3) \quad i\hbar \frac{\partial \Psi}{\partial t} = \sqrt{m^2 c^4 - (\hbar c)^2 \nabla^2} \Psi$$

By developing the root of the right side, you get an equation that is as follows:

$$(4) \quad E^2 = m^2 c^4 + c^2 p^2$$

From this equation, we obtain the wave equation:

$$(5) \quad \left(\frac{1}{c^2}\frac{\partial^2}{\partial t^2} - \nabla^2\right)\Psi = \left(\frac{mc}{\hbar}\right)^2 \Psi$$

---

[19] Planck's constant (1900) corresponds to the idea of the German physicist that light travels in packets that he called quanta and that later was called photons. The Planck constant expresses a relationship between (kg x m² and sec). Expresses a relationship between energy and time. The commonly accepted value for the constant is h = 6.6260693 (11) x10-34 joules / second. The Dirac constant divides the Planck constant by 2π. See. Lawkin, Kerwin (1968).

[20] The operator that associates with the energy in a physical system is a Hamiltonian operator, in honor of the Irish physicist William Rowan Hamilton (1805-1865). The Hamiltonian contains operations associated with the kinetic and potential energies. See. Lawkin, Kerwin (1968).

This equation is known as the Klein-Gordon equation. Dirac (1928) makes the decision to maintain the first temporal derivative along with the first spatial derivatives. This assumes the use of equation (1). The equation that emerges is then:

$$(6) \quad H = \alpha_0 mc^2 + \sum_{j=1}^{3} \alpha_j cp_j$$

Where, $p_j = -\frac{i\hbar \partial}{\partial x_j}$ the negative value of the root of -1 by the derived Dirac constant. These operators can be represented as matrices of size *nxn*, while ψ cannot be considered a scalar, but is a vector of n dimensions:

$$(7) \quad \psi(r,t) = \begin{pmatrix} \psi_1(r,t) \\ \cdot \\ \cdot \\ \cdot \\ \psi_n(r,t) \end{pmatrix}$$

This matrix is known as *spinor*[21]. An important contribution in relation with the importance of Dirac's theory can be found in the work of Plonitsky (2015). Plonitsky explains the development of the Dirac`s work in two main elements:

- First, the *influence of Heisenberg's* thinking, mainly the paper about the introduce tot the quantum mechanics.
- Second, the *transformation* theory especially important in the advantage to the study of the particles.

Approach for two productive factors

The following application is based on the important formulation proposed by Dirac (1928), and tries in some way, to approach an interaction between capital and work, trying to

---

[21] Thus, as it is observed that the earth revolves around its own axis (rotation) and around the sun (translation), the electron as an elementary particle, "orbits" around the atomic nucleus thanks to the electromagnetic field, but in turn, registers a movement on itself. This idea was developed in principle by Kronig, Goudsmit and Uhlenbeck. The electric field that generates electron when turning on its own axis is called spin and has been calculated thanks to the contributions of Dirac, based on the Planck constant divided by 2π. It is considered that the spins of several elementary particles correspond to the Dirac constant multiplied by integer and half-integer values.

contribute significantly to an advance in the understanding of the relationship between both factors.

Method

The methodology corresponds to a methodology of quantitative character, where data from the use of a productivity indicator that highlights two factors: capital and labor are analyzed. The study analyzes this indicator for eleven countries of different levels of development and analyzes -in a quantitative and transversal way, specifically for the level found by Aten, Heston & Summers (2002), Bernanke & Gürkaynak (2001), Barro & Lee (2000), for the year 2002-, the application of the proposed matrix as a comparison of these levels of interaction between these factors. On the other hand, it establishes levels of comparison between countries based on the equations proposed in section three of this article, to determine the relationship between reference countries, in this case the United States, and the other countries. For this, the following considerations are raised.

In principle, the existence of two (2) productive factors, namely, capital (K) and work (L)[22] will be assumed. We will suppose in addition that both factors will have exponential growths, in such a way that:

$$(1) \quad Q = [K^p + L^p]^{\frac{1}{p}}$$

Where:
Q = production level.
K = capital factor.
L = work factor.
p = exponential performance of the productive factors.

It is important here to introduce the following restriction. Bearing in mind that capital and labor will not be at any time and in any way efficient, neither in a *Paretian* sense, nor from the point of view of rational elections, the p-value, cannot be equal in any of the cases or greater than 1. Then:

$$(2) \quad Q = [K^p + L^p]^{\frac{1}{p}}$$

Subject to:

$$(3) \quad p < 1$$

---

[22] The mathematical problem raised by Dirac, is the following:

$$\sqrt{x^2 + y^2} = ax + by$$

Any other way, we can affirm that production is equal to a coefficient of return on capital, multiplied by said factor, added with a coefficient of labor yield multiplied by the labor factor. In such a way that we can express this second entity in the following way:

$$(4) \qquad Q = aK + bL$$

Where:
Q = production level.
a = capital yield coefficient.
K = capital factor.
b = work performance coefficient.
L = work factor

We will assume, moreover, that the coefficients of the yield of both factors represent their elasticity, but we will take into account, as in equation (v), that these elasticities will be lower than 1, since there is no intensive and efficient use of such factors. So:

$$(5) \qquad a < 1$$

$$(6) \qquad b < 1$$

Here, moreover, we will not assume its homogeneity as in the Cobb-Douglas equation. If we now equate equations (4) and (7), we will have the following expression:

$$(7) \qquad [K^p + L^p]^{\frac{1}{p}} = aK + bL$$

It could be affirmed so far that this equality implies increasing returns of capital and labor factors, but not efficient ones. Contrarily, we should introduce the following consideration in the model. The more significant the yields of labor and capital, the lower will be the yield of the sum of both factors in such a way that, if economies of scale are considered in the long term. However, we will pause at a moment in the following consideration. At some point, the use of factors would imply that returns, both capital and labor, will be equal to the joint yield of both factors.
If this is accepted, we will have the following situation for a growth of the productive factors with exponent two (2):

$$(8) \qquad [K^2 + L^2]^{\frac{1}{2}} = aK + bL$$

Can also be expressed by:

$$(9) \qquad \sqrt{K^2 + L^2} = aK + bL$$

This is precisely the expression of Dirac. For each of the cases of exponential growth equal to or greater than 2, we will have:

$$[K^3 + L^3]^{\frac{1}{3}} = aK + bL$$

$$[K^4 + L^4]^{\frac{1}{4}} = aK + bL$$

(10)

$$\vdots$$

$$[K^q + L^q]^{\frac{1}{q}} = aK + bL$$

For all q greater than 2.

$$(11) \qquad q > 2$$

We are now going to establish the solution for the situation in which the yields of the productive factors and the exponential increase of unclear both are considered as their squares, that is, as expressed in equation (13):

$$[K^2 + L^2]^{\frac{1}{2}} = aK + bL$$

If we assume that $aK + bL$, squared equals the sum of both factors raised to a growth exponent, we will have the following expression:

$$(12) \qquad K^2 + L^2 = (aK + bL)(aK + bL)$$

If we solve the right side of equality, we will have the following expression:

$$(13) \qquad K^2 + L^2 = a^2 K^2 + 2aKbL + b^2 L^2$$

That is, the sum of the squares of the productive factors are equivalent to the elasticity of capital squared and multiplied by the value of the factor also squared plus twice the multiplication of both elasticities and productive factors. Finally, the elasticity of work squared by the work factor squared is added.

In this direction, it is where the situation found is contradictory, since for the equation to be equal, it would mean that the elasticities of capital are both equal to 1 and that they are equal to 0, for the case of the expression 2aKbL. That is to say:

$$(14) \qquad a = b = 1$$

$$(15) \qquad a = b = 0$$

This is contradictory for the following assumptions or conditions. In the first place, that both elasticities cannot represent values a = b = 1 and a = b = 0; and on the other hand, the assumption that both elasticities are less than 1. In such a way, that it is not fulfilled that:

$$(16) \quad a < 1$$

$$(17) \quad b < 1$$

Here, the persistent appreciation of Dirac, acquires vital importance because we have to consider the following situation: suppose that the multiplication of the elasticities of both factors differs in the following way. The multiplication of the value of the elasticity of the labor value is different from the multiplication of the labor value by the elasticity of capital, that is to say[23]:

$$(18) \quad ab \neq ba$$

This level of abstraction, supposes locating us in another level, since if we return to the equation (13):

$$(19) \quad [K^2 + L^2]^{\frac{1}{2}} = aK + bL$$

We can express it in the following way:

---

[23] It is difficult to understand this assumption. Example of divergent thinking and contrary to any of the considerations on several of the numerical systems. I propose to understand this new level of analysis the following situation: we know in advance the evident separation that will be observed between water and oil when both substances are desired to be mixed. However, the behavior of the substances is not the same nor much less homogenous when the decision is made to introduce any of them in principle. There will be a whole series of unstable states between both substances until reaching the state of equilibrium. This allows us to understand that the relationship between introducing the oil in principle and introducing water in principle is not homogeneous. This assessment serves to understand the perspective of Dirac, by proposing in effect that a system or frame of reference could be found where the affectation of one variable over another, in this case ab, is different from the inverse relationship ba. The contradiction about the ownership of switching could be explored in many other systems. The great contribution of Dirac is, as we will see later, the fact of precisely finding a frame of reference in which this violation of the commutative law could occur. For Dirac (1967): "All observation consists of measuring a dynamic variable. From the physical point of view, it is evident that the result of such measurement must always be a real number, and thus we will suppose that any dynamic variable that we can measure must be a real dynamic variable. It may be thought that it would be possible to measure a complex dynamic variable by measuring its real part and its imaginary part separately, but this would involve two measurements or two observations. Although in classical mechanics it is possible, in quantum mechanics it is not, because in general, the measurements interfere with each other - it is not possible to admit that two observations are carried out exactly at the same time, and if they are made one after another in rapid succession, usually the first one alters the state of the system and introduces an indetermination that affects the second" (Dirac, 1967, p.46).

$$(20) \quad \sqrt{K^2 + L^2} = a^2 K^2 + KL(ab + ba) + b^2 L^2$$

That is a = 1; b = 1 and (ab + ba) = 0. For this to be accomplished, we will have to locate ourselves in the matrix algebra, namely, suppose that both a, and b, that is, the elasticities of both factors correspond to matrices. Consider a matrix expressed for an and b, such as:

$$(21) \qquad a = \begin{pmatrix} a_{11} & a_{12} \\ a_{21} & a_{22} \end{pmatrix} \qquad y \quad b = \begin{pmatrix} b_{11} & b_{12} \\ b_{21} & b_{22} \end{pmatrix}$$

For this pair of matrices, it is found that both elasticities have no solution. For a 3x3 matrix as follows:

$$(22) \quad a = \begin{pmatrix} a_{11} & a_{12} & a_{13} & a_{14} \\ a_{21} & a_{22} & a_{23} & a_{24} \\ a_{31} & a_{32} & a_{33} & a_{34} \\ a_{41} & a_{42} & a_{43} & a_{44} \end{pmatrix} \quad y \quad b = \begin{pmatrix} b_{11} & b_{12} & b_{13} & b_{14} \\ b_{21} & b_{22} & b_{23} & b_{24} \\ b_{31} & b_{32} & b_{33} & b_{34} \\ b_{41} & b_{42} & b_{43} & b_{44} \end{pmatrix}$$

The solution found for these two matrices is the following[24]:

$$(23) \quad a = \begin{pmatrix} 0 & 0 & 0 & 1 \\ 0 & 0 & 1 & 0 \\ 0 & 1 & 0 & 0 \\ 1 & 0 & 0 & 0 \end{pmatrix} \quad y \quad b = \begin{pmatrix} 1 & 0 & 0 & 0 \\ 0 & 1 & 0 & 0 \\ 0 & 0 & -1 & 0 \\ 0 & 0 & 0 & -1 \end{pmatrix}$$

If we now multiply the matrix a, the elasticity of capital by the capital factor, we will have[25]:

---

[24] If $a^2 = b^2 = 1$, then the matrix that expresses this solution is the identity matrix with 1 in its diagonal:

$$a = \begin{pmatrix} 1 & 0 & 0 & 0 \\ 0 & 1 & 0 & 0 \\ 0 & 0 & 1 & 0 \\ 0 & 0 & 0 & 1 \end{pmatrix} \quad y \quad b = \begin{pmatrix} 1 & 0 & 0 & 0 \\ 0 & 1 & 0 & 0 \\ 0 & 0 & 1 & 0 \\ 0 & 0 & 0 & 1 \end{pmatrix}$$

And if it is assumed that (ab + ba) = 0, then:

$$a = \begin{pmatrix} 0 & 0 & 0 & 0 \\ 0 & 0 & 0 & 0 \\ 0 & 0 & 0 & 0 \\ 0 & 0 & 0 & 0 \end{pmatrix} \quad y \quad b = \begin{pmatrix} 0 & 0 & 0 & 0 \\ 0 & 0 & 0 & 0 \\ 0 & 0 & 0 & 0 \\ 0 & 0 & 0 & 0 \end{pmatrix}$$

$$(24) \quad a = \begin{pmatrix} 0 & 0 & 0 & 1 \\ 0 & 0 & 1 & 0 \\ 0 & 1 & 0 & 0 \\ 1 & 0 & 0 & 0 \end{pmatrix} * K \quad = \begin{pmatrix} 0 & 0 & 0 & K \\ 0 & 0 & K & 0 \\ 0 & K & 0 & 0 \\ K & 0 & 0 & 0 \end{pmatrix}$$

Moreover, if we multiply the matrix b, that is, the elasticity of the labor factor, we will have:

$$(25) \quad b = \begin{pmatrix} 1 & 0 & 0 & 0 \\ 0 & 1 & 0 & 0 \\ 0 & 0 & -1 & 0 \\ 0 & 0 & 0 & -1 \end{pmatrix} * L \quad = \begin{pmatrix} L & 0 & 0 & 0 \\ 0 & L & 0 & 0 \\ 0 & 0 & -L & 0 \\ 0 & 0 & 0 & -L \end{pmatrix}$$

In this sense, the sum of the elasticities of the factors can be expressed as the sum of the matrices aK + bL, in the following way:

$$(26) \quad aK \quad = \begin{pmatrix} 0 & 0 & 0 & K \\ 0 & 0 & K & 0 \\ 0 & K & 0 & 0 \\ K & 0 & 0 & 0 \end{pmatrix} + bL = \begin{pmatrix} L & 0 & 0 & 0 \\ 0 & L & 0 & 0 \\ 0 & 0 & -L & 0 \\ 0 & 0 & 0 & -L \end{pmatrix}$$

In such a way that we obtain:

$$(27) \quad aK + bL = \begin{pmatrix} L & 0 & 0 & K \\ 0 & L & K & 0 \\ 0 & K & -L & 0 \\ K & 0 & 0 & -L \end{pmatrix}$$

Equation (13) can be expressed in terms of matrices as follows:

$$(28) \quad \sqrt{\begin{pmatrix} K^2+L^2 & 0 & 0 & 0 \\ 0 & K^2+L^2 & 0 & 0 \\ 0 & 0 & K^2+L^2 & 0 \\ 0 & 0 & 0 & K^2+L^2 \end{pmatrix}} = \begin{pmatrix} L & 0 & 0 & K \\ 0 & L & K & 0 \\ 0 & K & -L & 0 \\ K & 0 & 0 & -L \end{pmatrix}$$

This is equivalent to:

$$(29) \quad \begin{pmatrix} K^2+L^2 & 0 & 0 & 0 \\ 0 & K^2+L^2 & 0 & 0 \\ 0 & 0 & K^2+L^2 & 0 \\ 0 & 0 & 0 & K^2+L^2 \end{pmatrix} = \begin{pmatrix} L & 0 & 0 & K \\ 0 & L & K & 0 \\ 0 & K & -L & 0 \\ K & 0 & 0 & -L \end{pmatrix}^2$$

The determinant of the matrix $aK + bL$, is equivalent to:

$$(30) \quad Det = K^8 - 4K^6L^2 + 6K^4L^4 + 4K^2L^6 + L^8$$

Results and discussion

The following results are presented in two parts. In the first place, the result related to the application of the determinant based on Dirac is shown and in the second instance the coefficients underproduction by countries. In the following table, we find a numerical example of the countries referenced in the year 1998:

Country	Determinant[26] $(K^8 - 4K^6L^2 + 6K^4L^4 + 4K^2L^6 + L^8)$
United States	13
Canada	13,14
Japan	36,41
Finland	15,89
United Kingdom	2,73
South Korea	3,4
Mexico	0,31
Peru	0,34
India	0,04
Kenya	0,03
Tanzania	0,01

Table 17 Determinant of the interaction of the productive factors in relation to the United States 1998.

Is obvious, the importance of the position of Japan, Finland, Canada, and United States. Why have this difference with respect to *average underproduction?* The relative position of Japan with respect the other countries, is explain because the new level of physical capital per worker *(k)*, is affected directly the determinant. In the following graph, we attain the determinant for each of the cases, as observed Japan, Canada and Finland has a determinant of productive factors greater than the United States, which means a greater intensity in the use of both factors. Japan excels, with a determinant that almost triples that of States, but it has similar values for Finland and Canada.

---

[26] See the Appendix in the last part of the book. Mean STD and other statistical values.

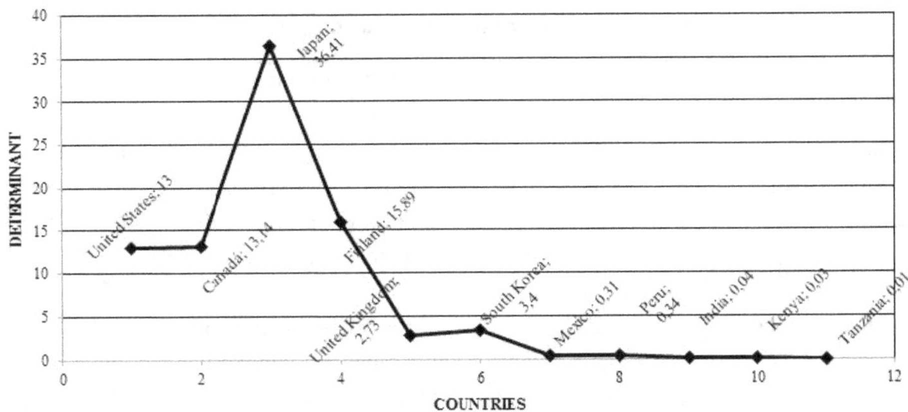

Figure 16 Values of the determinant of productive values for several countries 1998. Source: Own construction on the data of Aten, Heston & Summers (2002), Bernanke & Gürkaynak (2001), and Barro & Lee (2000).

With respect to the average for country, we have a set of countries for area in the world. For the case of North America, the results obtained are:

United States	*Average*	Canada	*Average*
United States/Canada	1,31	Canada/United States	0,76
United States/Japan	1,37	Canada/Japan	1,04
United States/Finland	1,41	Canada/Finland	1,07
United States/United Kingdom	1,42	Canada/United Kingdom	1,08
United States/South Korea	2,28	Canada/South Korea	1,61
United States/Mexico	3,13	Canada/Mexico	2,39
United States/Peru	4,93	Canada/Peru	3,76
United States/India	11,9	Canada/India	9,08
United States/Kenya	24,15	Canada/Kenya	18,41
United States/Tanzania	66,49	Canada/Tanzania	50,68

Table 18 Average two Countries North America. Source: Own construction

The position of United States with respect to Canada is better. In the area of Europa, the comparison between Finland and United Kingdom shows a relative better position to Finland.

Finland	*Average*	United Kingdom	*Average*
Finland/United States	0,71	United Kingdom/United States	0,7
Finland/Canada	0,93	United Kingdom /Canada	0,92
Finland/Japan	0,97	United Kingdom/Japan	0,97
Finland/United Kingdom	1,01	United Kingdom/Finland	0,99
Finland/South Korea	1,62	United Kingdom/South Korea	1,61
Finland/Mexico	2,23	United Kingdom/Mexico	2,21
Finland/Peru	3,5	United Kingdom/Peru	3,47
Finland/India	8,46	United Kingdom/India	8,39
Finland/Kenya	17,16	United Kingdom/Kenya	17,02
Finland/Tanzania	47,23	United Kingdom/Tanzania	46,86

Table 19 Average two countries of Europa. Source: Own construction

The position of Finland is advantageous with respect to the United Kingdom, South Korea, Mexico, Peru, India, Kenya and Tanzania, but disadvantage with respect to the United States, Canada and japan. The United Kingdom has a disadvantage with the United States, Canada, and Finland. In Asia, we find a best position in japan with respect to South Korea and India.

Japan	*Average*	South Korea	*Average*	India	*Average*
Japan/United States	0,73	South Korea/United States	0,44	India/United States	0,08
Japan/Canada	0,96	South Korea/Canada	0,58	India/Canada	0,11
Japan/Finland	1,03	South Korea/Japan	0,6	India/Japan	0,12
Japan/United Kingdom	1,04	South Korea/Finland	0,62	India/Finland	0,12
Japan/South Korea	1,66	South Korea/United Kingdom	0,62	India/ United Kingdom	0,12
Japan/Mexico	2,29	South Korea/Mexico	1,37	India/South Korea	0,19
Japan//Peru	3,6	South Korea/Peru	2,16	India/Mexico	0,26
Japan/India	8,69	South Korea/India	5,22	India/Peru	0,41
Japan/Kenya	17,63	South Korea/Kenya	10,59	India/Kenya	2,03
Japan Tanzania	48,54	South Korea/Tanzania	29,16	India/Tanzania	5,59

Table 20 Average three countries of Asia. Source: Own construction

In the zone, of South America the position for Mexico with respect to Peru. The fact of be nearest of the United States is an important factor in the dynamics of the interaction with the labor market and the foreign investment from the north.

Mexico	Average	Peru	Average
Mexico/United States	0,32	Peru/United States	0,2
Mexico/Canada	0,42	Peru/Canada	0,27
Mexico/Japan	0,44	Peru/Japan	0,28
Mexico/Finland	0,45	Peru/Finland	0,29
Mexico/United Kingdom	0,45	Peru/ United Kingdom	0,29
Mexico/South Korea	0,73	Peru/South Korea	0,46
Mexico/Peru	2,1	Peru/Mexico	0,64
Mexico/India	3,8	Peru/India	2,41
Mexico/Kenya	7,71	Peru/Kenya	4,9
Mexico/Tanzania	21,21	Peru/Tanzania	13,48

Table 21 Average two countries of South America. Source: Own construction

Finally, the comparison between Tanzania and Kenya is advantageous for the second nation.

Tanzania	Average	Kenya	Average
Tanzania/United States	0,02	Kenya/United States	0,04
Tanzania/Canada	0,02	Kenya/Canada	0,05
Tanzania/Japan	0,02	Kenya/Japan	0,06
Tanzania/Finland	0,02	Kenya/Finland	0,06
Tanzania/United Kingdom	0,02	Kenya/United Kingdom	0,06
Tanzania/South Korea	0,03	Kenya/South Korea	0,09
Tanzania/Mexico	0,05	Kenya/Mexico	0,13
Tanzania/Peru	0,07	Kenya/Peru	0,2
Tanzania/India	0,18	Kenya/India	0,49
Tanzania/Kenya	0,36	Kenya/Tanzania	2,75

Table 22 Average two countries of Africa. Source: Own construction

Really, the differences between countries lead to a reality, probably already known and that constitutes a working hypothesis in front of the situation of development and progress of different countries in the incorporation of factors such as work and capital, but the fundamental differences with respect to traditional measurement approaches are based on the fact of articulating these measurements to other interdisciplinary areas and for this, intercountry comparisons and the determinant provide elements to be considered as the Finnish advantage and the Japanese advantage.

References

Arrow Kenneth J, *Chenery* H B, *Minhas* B S & *Solow* Robert. (1961). Capital-labor substitution and economic efficiency. Rev. Econ. Statist. 43:225-50

Aten, Bettina, Heston, Alan, & Summers, Robert (2002). Penn World Table Version 6.1. Center for International Comparisons. University of Pennsylvania (CICUP).

Barro, Robert, J. & Jong-Wha Lee. (2000). "International Data on Educational Attainment: Updates and Implications". *Oxford Economic Papers,* 53(3) July: 541-563.

Bernanke, Ben & Gürkaynak, Refet, S. (2001). *Is growth Exogenous? Taking Mankiw, Romer and Weil seriously*. MIT.Press.

Bjorken, James, D. & Drell, Sidney, D. (1964). *Relativistic Quantum Mechanics.* McGraw-Hill.

Cobb, C.W. & Douglas, Paul. H. (1928). "A Theory of Production". *American Economic Review* 18 (supplement): 139-165.

Cobb, C. W. & Douglas, Paul. H. (1948). "Are there Laws of Production?". *The American Economic Review* 38: 1-41.

Contreras, Ana, María. & Larralde, Hernán. (2013). *Econofísica*. En: Fronteras de la Física en el siglo XXI. Miramontes, Octavio. & Volke, Karen (Editores). Coplt-arXives. Mexico D.F.

Cottingham, Noel & Greenwood, Dereck, A. (1998). *An introduction to the Standard Model of Particle Physics*. Cambridge University Press.

Dirac, Paul. (1928). *The Quantum Theory of the Electron*. St. John's College, Cambridge. (Communicated by R.H. Fowler, F.R.S.- Received January 2, 1928.

Dirac, Paul. (1968). *Principios de mecánica Cuántica*. Ed. Ariel. España.

Douglas. Paul, H. (1934). *The Theory of Wages*. New York. The Macmillan Co.

Fisher, F. M. (1992). *Aggregation. Aggregate Production Functions and Related Topics*. Cambridge, MA: The MIT Press.

Lawkin, Kerwin (1968). *Introducción a la Física Atómica*. Ed. Norma.

Lucas, Robert. (2002). *Lecturas sobre crecimiento económico*. Grupo Editorial Norma y Uniandes.

Mandl, Franz & Shaw, Graham. (1986). *Quantum Field Theory*. John Wiley & Sons.

Mankiw, N. George. (2004). *Macroeconomía: 93-96*. Antoni Bosch editor.

Mantegna, Rosario, N. & Stanley, H. Eugene. (2000). *An Introduction to Econophysics*. Cambridge University Press.

Mayumi, K, Giampetro, M, & Ramos-Martín, J. (2012). "Reconsideration of dimensions and curve fitting practice in view of Georgescu-Roegen's epistemology in Economics". *Romanian Journal of Economic Forecasting,* 4: 17-35.

Nicholson, Walter. (2007). *Teoría Microeconómica. Principios básicos y ampliaciones*. 9 Ed. Ed. Thomson.

Ormerod, Paul (2010). "Econophysics and The Social Sciences: Challenges and Opportunities". *Journal of Natural and cultural sciences.* 76: 345-35.

Plotnitsky, Arkady. (2015). "A Matter of Principle: The principles of Quatum Theory, Dirac's Equation, and Quantum Information". *Foundations of Physics.* 1-39. DOI: 10.1007/s10701-015-9929-z

Prescott, Edward. (1986). "Theory ahead of business cycle measurement". *Federal Reserve Bank of Minneapolis Quarterly Review*: 9-22.

Samuelson, Paul & Nordhaus William. (2010). *Economía con aplicaciones a Latinoamérica*. 19 ed. Ed. Mac Graw Hill.

Stanley, H. E., Amarala, L.A.N. Gabaixb, X. Gopikrishnana, P. Pleroua, V. (2001) "Similarities and differences between physics and economics". *Physica A* 299: 1–15

Solow, Robert, M. (1957). "Technical Change and the Aggregate Production Function". *Review of Economics and Statistics* 39: 312-320.

Soler, Yezid. (s.f). *Diálogos de la Economía con otras ciencias.* Asociación de Economistas de la Universidad Nacional de Colombia (AEUN). Facultad de Ciencias Económicas.

Sylos-Labini, Paolo. (1995). "Why the interpretation of the Cobb-Douglas production function must be radically changed". *Structural Change & Ec. Din.* 6:485-504.

Varian, Hal. (1998). *Microeconomía intermedia un enfoque actual.* 4 ed. Ed. Antoni Bosch. Barcelona España.

CHAPTER 4

THEORY OF THE PORTFOLIO IN THE SHORT TERM: THE CASE OF A BASKET OF THREE SHARES

Recognizing the importance that the advances in the mix of different investment options have had in the last three decades, it could be said that those advances are mainly due to the recognition of *diversification* as an essential element in the reduction of risk, in the categorization of types of risk faced by entrepreneurs and empirical evidence in the different stock market data that are matched with theoretical approaches that will allow efficient decision making. That is why, the theory of the portfolio can provide relevant elements in the understanding of profitability expectations and especially for the Colombian case, a basket of shares combined of a businessman as a *rational agent* he seeks two basic objectives: to reduce the risk and to maximize profitability.

Taking into account the previous elements, it is important to bear in mind that the Theory of the Portfolio (TP) presents two fundamental elements: one of them is the intertemporality which means, the relationship that the stock exchange data have, period by period in terms of their changes or variations, their central tendency measures and the dispersion of them. In the other hand, the other fundamental element is the uncertainty that refers mainly to the absence of complete information that allows the investor to make an appropriate decision according to the margins of desired profitability.

The objective of this paper is to propose an investment portfolio consisting of a basket of three (3) investments from companies belonging mainly to the mining and energy sector of Colombia and listed on the Colombian Stock Exchange (CSE), as a basic element for business decision making. However, it is necessary to contextualize the topic in terms of its historical development and its progress. It is also necessary to clarify the quantitative elements that allow the understanding of the internal interaction of the portfolio.

Some Historical Data

Markowitz (1952) presents a portfolio analysis of nine North American companies from 1937 to 1955. This is made to define the return of portfolios; the author uses the following expression:

(1)   *Returns = (closing price t) – (closing price t-1) + (dividends t/ closing price t-1)*

It can be defined as:

R = (Return on investment or profitability).

CLt = Closing price in period t.

CLt-1 = Closing price in period t-1.

D = Dividends in the period t.

The definition of dividends can be made in three different models: a first growth model that considers that the dividends on the shares of a company depend on profitability exclusively (p); this model for Court and Tarradellas (2008), is called the discounted dividend model zero sum. Another model considers that the dividends depend, in addition, on the profitability of the market price of the stock and a constant growth gradient (g). This model is called constant yield model or Gordon model and finally the growth model of multiple dividends, which is considered like:

> ... for a certain number of years, indicated as *T*, the growth of dividends will not have a constant growth pattern, but after this period, the investor will assume a specific pattern of growth (Court and Tarradellas, 2008, p. 48).

These methods allow both the definition of the calculation of dividends and the market price of the shares and they are based precisely on specific market shares of a single company, therefore they only allow, at first, the analysis of a single type of shares. The reality of the investor implies that he can design a basket of investments that may include stocks, fixed income investments, bonds, financial derivatives, and elements that include in the portfolio investments in the *Forex* market. In this study particularly, it is considered that the portfolio is composed of a basket of shares of three (3) traditional companies listed on the CSE. Then, some theoretical aspects about PT will be addressed.

Theoretical aspects of TP

The importance of this paradigmatic advance in the study of investment mechanisms lies in the use of statistical measurement tools that allow an accurate decision-making about assets that generate disparate returns:

> ... The theory of the portfolio can be defined as a method of determining optimal decisions about behavior of assets and certainty (Romero, 2010, p.106).

There are two key elements in TP in its modern version. For Hirshleifer and Riley (2002), it is considered that the decision making under uncertainty, for example the decision of choice between shares or investment prospects, have to do with probability distributions that generally associate a quantity of consumption (in this case, it would be the choice of investment options), as a contingent in each *state of nature* with the degree of belief (usually measured as a probability), that such a state occurs. This is an approach that for the authors:

> ... postulates that, for any individual, the probability distribution associated with any prospect is effectively represented by only two statistical measures: the mean and the income deviation (Hirshleifer & Riley, 2002, p. 69).

In modern finance there are three fields of study which financial theory works on: the valuation of financial assets in the context of uncertainty, the efficient way of making decisions in the uncertain international environment and, the efficient organization and regulation of financial markets (Romero, 2010, p.106) It is important to have a general definition of an asset. This concept generally refers to the set of assets or rights that a company can own and that is registered in its accounting balance. According to Malagón (2006), for a good to be considered as an asset of a company does not necessarily need to be owned. The assets can be defined in the following types:

Fixed Asset.	Intangible Asset.	Liquid Asset	Tangible Asset
Another name that receives this asset is fixed *assets* and refers to the part of the asset that is made by the assets and *long-term rights* that are used by a company or firm for the fulfillment of the objectives in financial, economic terms and social. In other words, they correspond *to tangible and intangible goods, which* have a duration longer than the productive cycle. Some examples of it can be machinery, long-term deposits, and furniture, among others.	An intangible asset is immaterial, which is considered in the balance sheet of the company. They can be included in this category: patents, knowledge, trademarks, any right or good that the company has that may be of an immaterial nature.	It corresponds to the asset that can be easily converted into currency. Its conception is based on the theory of preference for *liquidity*. Among these are bank accounts, cash balances and short-term investments.	It is the part of the assets of the company with a physical or material representation. For mentioning some of them: buildings, machinery, and equipment, among others.

Table 23 Classification of assets. Source: Malagón (2006)

Based on the preference for liquidity, it could be said that *rational agents* - in this case, the businesspersons - will prefer those assets that can easily be made cash. For Nicholson (2007), individuals as rational agents will be willing to pay a certain amount of money to avoid *uncertainty*. This occurs due to the measure of sacrifice depends on the attitudes of the employer against the risk. In this sense, the relationships between a group of individuals or entrepreneurs will generate a set of risks in which the uncertainty can be reduced to a relatively satisfactory measure, if a price is paid for this reduction. The problem, in a quantitative point of view, will be to find the risk values and the analysis of the fixing of that price.

The best models that can explain the price analysis and the risk calculation is those related to the study of the *price of assets*. In those models, it is mainly analyzed the relationship between the return (expected return) of an asset and the associated risk with this type of return or profitability. At the historical level in the field of finance, it is interesting to mention as contributions to the theory of risk to Francis Galton (1875), who:

> ... Discovered the concept of *regression to made-to-measure*, which refers to, even if the prices fluctuate in organized markets and the assets are traded in those markets, they may be overvalued or undervalued. In addition, they will tend to historical prices average, arriving consequently to the averaged normality that they have always shown (Rosillo & Martínez, 2004, p 16)[27].

Another fundamental contribution was made by Tobin (1972), who focused on the compensation that investors receive when they seek a triple balance between risks, benefits, and liquidity. In this sense the author's proposal mainly focuses on the action of governments (as regulatory authorities), that should concentrate on the creation of a tax rate for the collection of foreign currency transactions. This governmental action would reduce speculation and facilitate free trade. These contributions do not include the perspective of the combination of different types of investment yet. The Harry Markowitz's (1990) work has to do with the cumulative action of the assets in the portfolios, which is inversely proportional to the risk. This concept was called *diversification of portfolios*. The main and most important measure related to diversification has to do with the dispersion of the assets which make part of it, mainly the standard deviation (σ). Other important elements in Markowitz's approach have to do with covariance and correlation. If a set of assets in a portfolio are negatively correlated, the risk will be lower. For Markowitz (1952), the concepts of utility or benefit are equally important.

The TP has also advanced from the contributions of Sharpe (1990), who establishes a pricing model for financial assets in which entrepreneurs have the option to choose a so-called *exposure to risk*, by combining fixed-rate securities and variable-rate securities. In

---

[27] In this theorization, it is notorious the influence of the Physiocratic economists that has to do with the notion of *natural equilibrium*.

this case, if an optimal composition of the portfolio is desired, it depends on the valuation that the investors give to the *perspectives* that could be associated to the theory of rational expectations that the assets are presumed they will have and won't their attitude towards risk. For Rosillo & Martínez (2004), this is what is called systematic risk. On the other hand, Sharpe (1990), in his proposals, introduces the concept of the Securities Market Lines or SML.

The problem that Markowitz formulated has to do with the investor's rational choice of a stock market. In the beginning, not much attention was given to this problem since the stock market had little influence in the financial market. Then, there were few significant advances in the use of computer methods (Romero, 2010, pag, 110). A fundamental axiom must be considered: The investor considers desirable the expected return but undesirable the variance of those returns (Romero, 2010, p. 111). The variance of the portfolio can be defined as the current performance of the assets. To understand these concepts, certain definitions of statistics must be considered respect to the dispersion of both returns and prices in the stock market. Here are some considerations.

Authors such as Freund (1992) and Hoel (1984) have presented deeper developments. The return on financial assets (x_i) presents a normal distribution. The average of (x_i) (μ_i) indicates the expected return of the asset i.

On the other hand, it is important to know the income function that the investor expects and that is expressed through the first two moments in which the capital is returned. A diversification model that is considered efficient maximizes the income function that the investor expects within a probable set of portfolios. This restriction shows that the investor consumes the capital they have available.

Concept of risk

To measure the degree of influence that an action can have, if it is acquired a well-diversified portfolio, it is necessary to measure the risk. As it was mentioned earlier in the risk typology (Rosillo & Martínez, 2004), the market risk is the most important. The sensitivity of the return, in the case of an investment conformed of a set of shares, is usually denominated with the value of β.

For Rosillo & Martínez (2004), the risk is an inherent element of any process that involves making decisions and, for the specific case of finance, it is related to potential losses that a portfolio of investments could have with a deductible return but that represents a variable income. Generally, the risk division mainly focuses on two major categories: non-diversifiable and diversifiable. The characteristics of each of these categories are presented below:

Systemic or non-diversifiable	Non-systemic or diversifiable
It refers to some factors that are external to corporations, such as economic policy measures, macroeconomic variables, and the international economy.	It is related to the behavior of the corporation in both, its interior and its external relationships. It is determined by variables such as management capacity, level of indebtedness, technological improvements, and financial risks.

Table 24 Types of risk from a structural position. Source: Rosillo & Martínez (2004)

On the other hand, the risk is defined in terms of return-risk and risk return. In the case of *return-risk*, the return is measured by the weighted average of the expected returns of the component values and the risk is measured by the variance of the asset and more specifically by the standard deviation (σ). Regards to the return risk, the investor must face a decision that implies the search of the highest level of expected return of the investment according to a level of risk that is presented. One way to reduce this risk is through the diversification of the portfolio, through a procedure called *efficient structuring of assets*. Respect to this, a weighting of each asset in the portfolio must be carried out, as well as calculating the variance or standard deviation of each asset, calculating the covariance or the correlation coefficient for each pair of values. Rosillo & Martínez (2004) classified the risks in ten (10) groups:

• **Market risk:** It corresponds to the probability of being affected by macroeconomic factors, which have to do with prices, interest rates, exchange rates, inflation, devaluation and some aspects that may make difficult the payment by the issuer or whoever is the guarantor of the portfolio. It could be considered as a systemic risk.

• **Liquidity Risk:** It has to do with the situations whereby economic agents must face situations in which the cash flows that are expected do not obey or generate cash flows. It produces at the same time lack of attention to previous compromises. It also has to do with the scarcity of the market to meet the existing portfolio offering and portfolios.

• **Legal Risk:** It has to do with the possibility of changing rules that may affect the parties involved. It is also associated with the presence of lawsuits between parties.

• **Operational Risk:** It is related to failures in the handling of information either voluntarily or involuntarily.

• **Inflation risk:** it is related to the loss of purchasing power of investment flows due to changes or variations in a country's inflation that end up affecting expectations against some performance. To make short-term estimates, for example Fixed Term Deposit

Certificates, bank acceptances, investment funds, it is important to include in the projected value the pertinent considerations related to the inflation.[28]

• **Interest risk:** this refers to the effect that variation in interest rates in the market can have on the flow. There is an inverse relationship between the interest rate and the value of the portfolio. The higher the interest rate, the value of the portfolio will be lower and the lower the interest rate the value of the portfolio will be higher.

• **Foreign exchange risk:** The foreign exchange risk is related to the exchange rate or the value of the main currencies in the market whether the investments have been made in currencies other than the national currency.

• **Solvency risk:** it is also the financial or credit risk and it corresponds to the level of uncertainty that the issuing party has of a financial obligation for the payment of interest or for the capital amortization.

• **Country risk:** it involves the dynamics and problems of a territory, due to political, social, religious, or economic effects that envisage a risky scenario for investors.

In addition to the risk classification, the need to perform a technical analysis is presented to the investor. Risk analysis is an essential element of the investment decision. There are some trends with respect to risk analysis below:

Risk Analysis

For the risk analysis, some methods can be used, both qualitatively and quantitatively. Identifying the risk allows to reduce the uncertainty regarding the decision-making process. If there is a risk scenario, its quantification is important. For example, through the assignment of probabilistic values. In this topic, Fiorito (2006) considers the existence of two approaches to the quantitative risk analysis: the analytical approach and the quantitative simulation approach.

This first approach has to do with the obtaining of descriptive information from the mathematical point of view and it requires a level of formal analysis that involves the use of basic statistics (average of central tendency, dispersion, and functions -mainly linear-, to obtain the projections and calculation of β). The second one has to do with the need to make use of statistical tools such as simulators and software's for complex calculations.

However, it is essential to take into account a complex elaboration of the entire economic and even social environment in which the portfolio is developed due to there are a multiplicity of factors that can significantly affect, and moreover by passing the time, the

---

[28] In the mid and long term, they can be done using indexed rates.

possible profitability and the breach of the expectations and goals of the portfolio. In the first moment, a context must be defined in which a risk management policy can be generated, including the verification of the existence of an adequate evaluation of each of one. That would address to the definition of the probabilistic point of view about which ones would be the most frequent and therefore which variables could be simulated.

Considering the type of distribution, the risk of a portfolio can be associated to the Beta β concept. For Rappaport (1986), β is defined as the volatility of the return of a role face a market portfolio. This rate of return is related to a security or value, which is derived from the appreciation of market value and dividends. There are a set of assumptions. The first is that this rate fluctuates according to the market, in this the β is 1.This shows that if there is a growth of 10% in the return of the market, an action will also react with a growth in its return of 10%. If on the other hand, this same action rises or falls by 5% when the market rises or falls 2.5%, β is 2. The β, allows establishing the degree of sensitivity of the profitability of a share face the variation of the stock market. For Pinilla, Valero and Guzmán (2007), it is expressed as the relationship between the covariance of the performance of the share and the performance of the market portfolio with the variance of the performance of the market portfolio. This value measures the systematic or non-diversifiable risk that has to do with aspects related to inflation, recessions, wars, variations in interest rates. From the statistical point of view, it is a linear regression[29] that is also called the *characteristic line of the stock market*. Its result can be interpreted as the degree of response of the variability of the performance of the share regards to the variability of market returns.

It can be said that the risk of the shares is strongly related to the market risk. The value of βi allows foreseeing the best combinations between them. A portfolio made by shares of high β is riskier than the one that is constituted with shares of lower β. That brings the principle that the risk of a well-diversified portfolio depends on the average β of the roles that it includes. In Latin American countries, in the absence of a well-developed capital market, the prices of shares have not been fully moved, they have moved in order to satisfy the tax needs of their owners, it used to be constituted by economic groups that hold most of the companies, under the protectionist economic model. (Gutiérrez, 1992), p. 325). Next, the empirical evidence will be presented in the case of the combination of shares of the companies Ecopetrol, Pacific Rubiales and Paz Del Río in the first semester of 2016.

---

[29] A formalization of the linear regression model can be found in Dhrymes (1994):

$$yt= xt\beta+ ut, \ t=1,2, 3, T \ [1]\}$$

yt is the dependent variable and the elements of 1 x (n + 1) of the vector column **xt**, are the independent variable or *explanatory*. The vector column consists of a set of unknown parameters whose estimation is reversed to the previous theory. Often, the variables in **xt** are called *regressors* and **yt** the **regressand** variable. (Dhrymes, 1994, p. 1).

Empirical evidence

In the following chart, it can be observed the variation of the share's prices of ECOPETROL from January to July 2016.

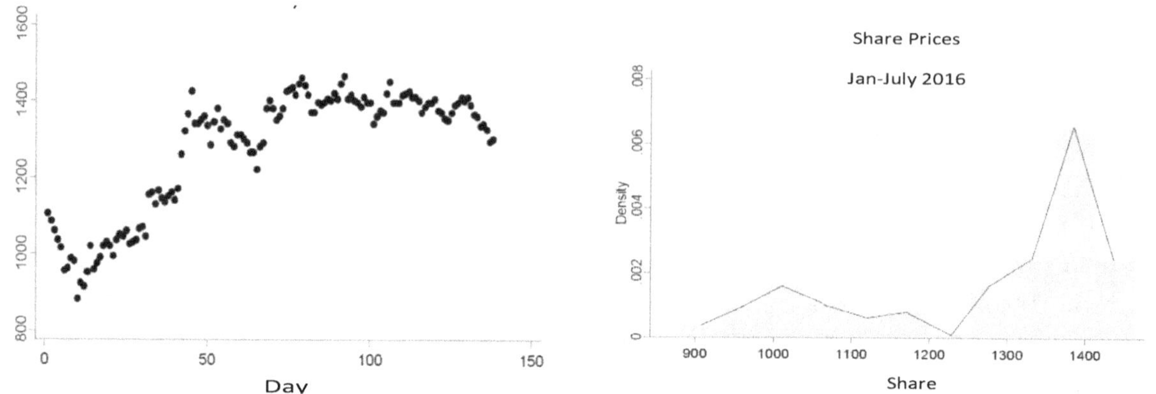

Figure 17 Shares prices Ecopetrol January- July 2016. Source: Own construction.

 The following graph shows the variation data smoothed through a Kernel[30] distribution, with a higher density of the data in ranges of prices of the shares are from 1.300 to 1.500 pesos, getting a density of 0.004, while the range of shares values from 900 and 1100 pesos have low-density ranges of 0.001.

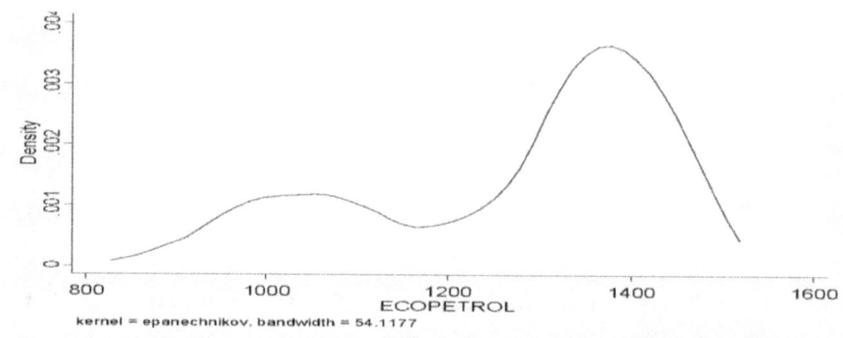

Figure 18 Kernel Density Estimate Ecopetrol. Source: Own construction.

---

[30] If there is a set *(X1, X2, ..., Xn)* that shows a set of size *n* that corresponds to a variable with density *f.* the Kernel density estimate of *f* to a point of *X*, it corresponds or it is given by:

$$fh'x=1nh \ i=1nK \ x-Xih \ (1)$$

Source: Sheater, 2004, pag, 588.

The range of variation for this type of shares did not present volatilities despite the worldwide drops in the price of oil[31]. It can be said that the slope of the function indicates that the average of the shares per day is $ 3,287459 and the shares value, that is independent of the daily variation corresponds to $ 1046,065.

$$(1) \; y = 1046,06 + 3,28459x$$

In the graphic below, it can be observed the variation of the share's prices of the company Paz del Río, in the time series and throughout the period studied.

Figure 19 Shares prices Paz del Rio January- July 2016. Source: Own construction.

The next graphic shows the variation data smoothed through a Kernel distribution showing a higher density in the ranges between $ 7.5 and $ 8.5 with densities of 0.3 and 0.4. On the other hand, the range of stock prices between $ 9 and $ 10 have low density:

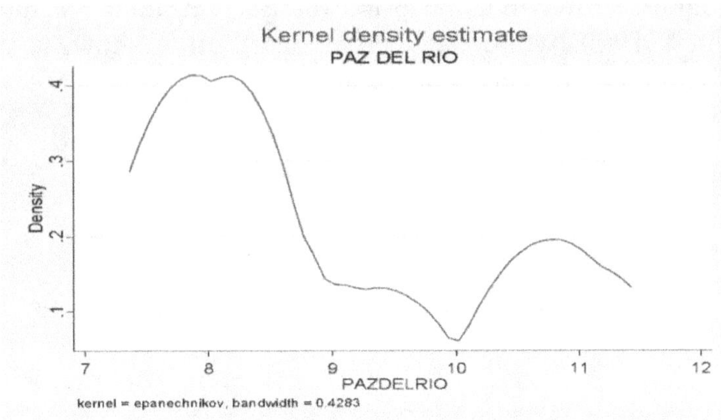

Figure 20 Kernel Density Estimate Paz del Río. Source: Own construction.

---

[31] This impact seems to be represented in the mid and long term, but not in the time series analyzed yet.

The number of observations is 141 and the minimum price of the share in the time series is $ 7.79 and maximum of $ 11 per share. The slope of the function indicates that the average variation of the shares per day corresponds to a decrease in its price of $ 0.0026312 and the price of the shares that is independent of the daily variation corresponds to $ 9.089087.

$$(2) \quad y = 9,089087 - 3,287459x$$

In the chart below, it could be observed the variation and the results of the prices of the shares of Pacific Rubiales for the same time series:

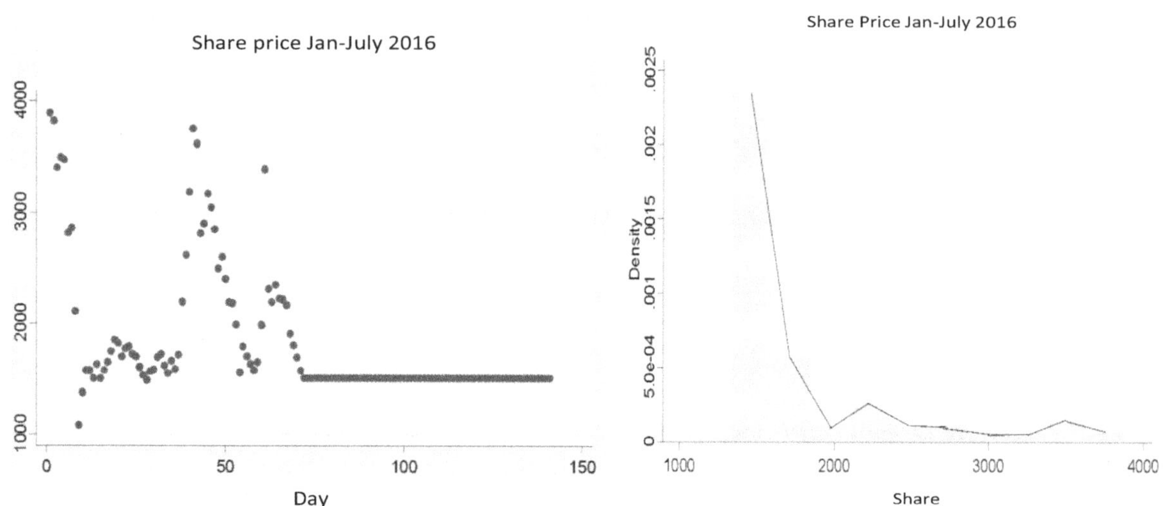

Figure 21Shares prices Paz del Rio Pacific Rubiales January- July 2016. Source: Own construction.

The frequency histogram shows that the price that is presented the most is in the range between $ 1400 and $ 1900, while the Kernel distribution shows a concentration with densities between 0 and 0.025 for the same values.

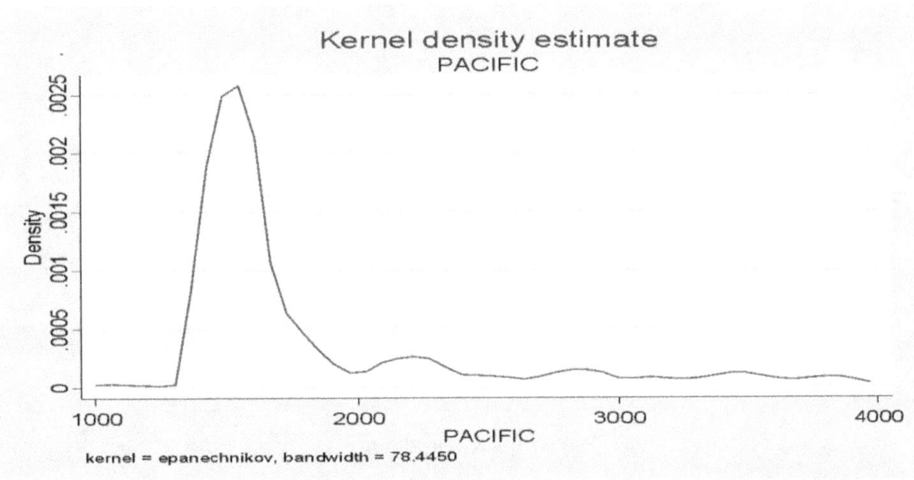

Figure 22 Kernel Density Estimate Paz del Río. Source: Own construction.

The number of observations is 141. The analysis shows that the change in the price of the share for one day is a loss of value of - $ 7.1275 with an equity value of $ 2333,821 that is independent of the variation of time.

$$(3) \quad y = 2333,821 - ,127531x$$

It is observed that the shares present greater volatility in the company PACIFIC, because a much higher price is obtained in their standard deviation related to the values found in the other two companies. On the other hand, PAZ DEL RÍO, and PACIFIC present, according to the trend, a reduction in the price per day, which matches to the value of the β (betas) corresponding to -0.0026 and -7.1275, respectively. In the case of ECOPETROL, there is a growth in the value of β, which corresponds to 3,2894. Unlike the trends of companies with negative β (betas), ECOPETROL presents a proportional increase of its daily value of the stock for the value. For the investor, these data are because they allow establishing investment decisions that will favor a greater proportion of purchase of these shares in the portfolio basket. The dual analysis, which corresponds to the integration of companies, it is presented below. The following graphic shows the behavior of the value of the shares of the company ECOPETROL, which is located on the coordinate and of the company PAZ DEL RIO, which is located on the abscissa.

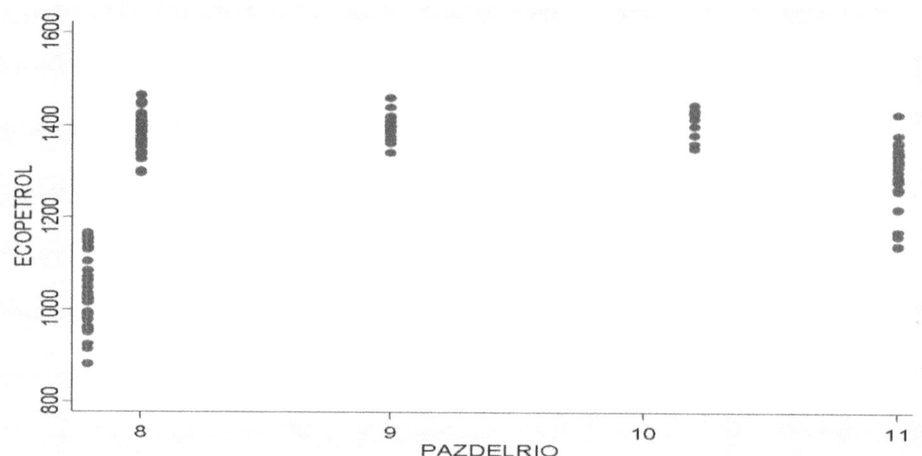

Figure 23 Shares prices Ecopetrol- Paz del Rio January- July 2016. Source: Own construction.

A linear regression was done between the values of stock prices for each company[32]. The correlation index in this case the *R - squared* is low 0.1275, which represents a low level of association between the prices of both companies. On the other hand, the function that defines the relationship between both prices is as follows:

$$(4)\ y = 5,319815 + 0,0028262x$$

If the prices of the share of ECOPETROL are varied by one unit, a change in the price of the PAZ DEL RÍO share will be expected, much less than one COP, which is in this case to 0.002826. In the same way, to scan the argument that could consider that the place of the shares of PAZ DEL RIO determine the value of ECOPETROL.

An inverse linear function was done to the previous one. In this case, it was considered that the variation in the prices of the RIO PAZ share would influence the value of the ECOPETROL share. It is observed for this case that the type of linear function that determines this relationship is the following:

$$(5)\ y = 871,8929 + 45,1306x$$

A variation in one unit of the price in the share of PAZ DEL RIO generates an increase in the value of the ECOPETROL share of $ 45, 13067. A regression was done that related the prices of ECOPETROL shares versus of PACIFIC RUBIALES. It is found the graphic that relates the price of the shares of both companies that present levels of dispersion much wider than the previous regression.

---

[32] It should be noted that the dates in which there was no coincidence in the stock exchange for both companies were eliminated.

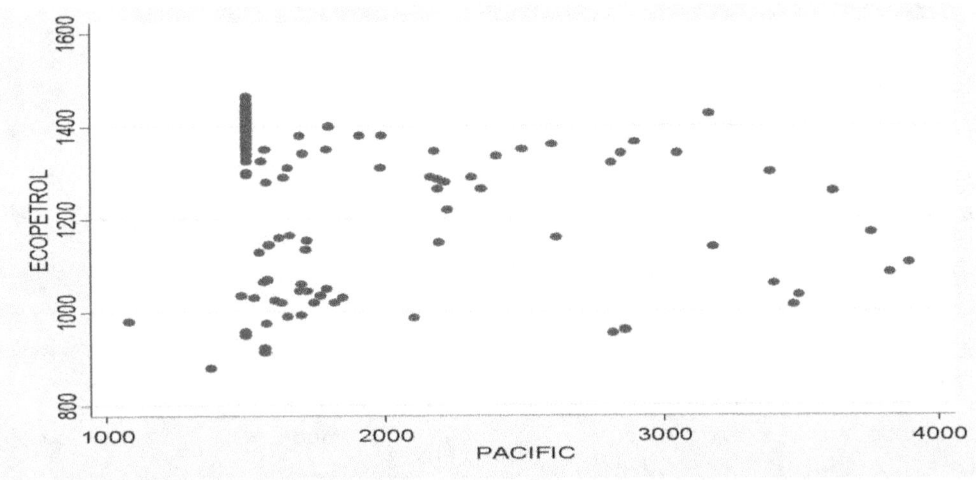

Figure 24 Shares prices Ecopetrol- Pacific Rubiales January- July 2016. Source: Own construction.

In the table, it can be found the results obtained. In this case, it is presented a very low correlation between both shares of less than 10%, which implies a low level of association between the prices of the shares of both companies.

On the other hand, based on the previous assumption that the shares of ECOPETROL depend on the variation in the price of the shares of PACIFIC, it is found that the variation in the price of the shares of PACIFIC generates a decrease in the value of the shares of -0 , 07166, while the independent value of ECOPETROL shares is $ 1406,041. The linear type function that expresses this relationship is the following:

$$(6) \quad y = 1406,041 - 0,016691x$$

In the inverse case, it is found that a variation in the shares of ECOPETROL generates a decrease in the price of the shares that is -0.9778884, while the price that is independent of the value of the shares of ECOPETROL is of $ 3081, 144. Subsequently, a simple regression was done based on the relationship between the companies PAZ DEL RIO and PACIFIC. Below, there are the data that show that relationship. The share price of PAZ DEL RIO does not suffer large variations with relatively low prices. The variation in prices in PACIFIC is much more significant.

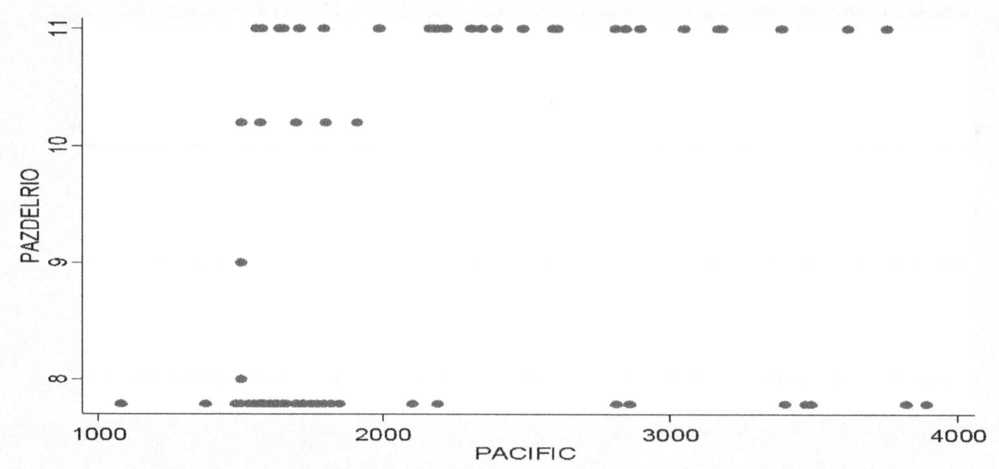

Figure 25 Shares prices Paz Del Río- Pacific Rubiales January- July 2016. Source: Own construction.

The correlation coefficient *R - squared* is relatively low with a value 13.04%, which indicates a poor association between the prices of both companies. Based on the consideration that investments in shares in PAZ DEL RIO, they are dependent on investments in PACIFIC shares, it seems that a variation in the price of PACIFIC shares generates an increase in the price of shares which is 0 , 0007753, while the independent price of the shares of PAZ DEL RIO, or that does not depend on the price of the shares of PACIFIC, is \$ 7,485278.

$$(7) \; y = 7,485278 + 0,00053x$$

In the same way, it was done an inverse linear regression that shows the following data. A variation in one unit in the share price of PAZ DEL RIO generates an increase in the price of PACIFIC shares of COP 168, 1463, while the price of shares of PACIFIC present a price of COP 330.8825, which is independent of the variation in the price of the shares of PAZ DEL RIO. Next, the obtained data are presented:

$$(8) \; y = 330,8825 + 168,1463x$$

Most of the *R - squared* correlation coefficients show low levels of association between the values of the shares of the three (3) companies, which reach 13%. On the other hand, most of the linear functions show positive slopes that show that a change in the actions of one of the companies will generate changes, -but significant-, at least positive in the other company. Based on these data, the covariance matrix is calculated for the three (3) companies presented below:

	PAZ DEL RIO	PACIFIC
PAZ DEL RIO	1,0000	
PACIFIC	0,3610	1,0000
	ECOPETROL	PACIFIC
ECOPETROL	1,0000	
PACIFIC	-0,2647	1,0000
	ECOPETROL	PAZ DEL RIO
ECOPETROL	1,0000	
PAZ DEL RIO	0,3571	1,0000

Table 25 Covariance matrix. Source: Own construction

Referencies

Brealy, R.A, Myers, S.C. (2006): *Principios de Finanzas Corporativas*. Ed. McGraw Hill.

Dhrymes, P. (1994). *Topics in advanced Econometrics Volume II. Linear and Nonlinear Simultaneous Equations*. Springer-Verlag. New York.

Fiorito, F. (2006). *La Simulación como una herramienta para el manejo de la incertidumbre*. Universidad del CEMA. Mayo 2006. http://www.ucema.edu.ar/u/ffiorito/Hand out_Simulacion_y_RISK_06.pdf

Gutiérrez, L. (1992). *Finanzas prácticas para países en desarrollo*. Ed. Norma. Bogotá. Colombia.

Hirshleifer, J, Riley, J. (2002). *The analytics of uncertainty and information*. Cambridge University Press.

Malagón, J. (2006). *Glosario Económico de Colombia*. Portafolio Glosario Económico de Colombia. Bogotá.

Medina, L, Á. (2003). "Aplicación de la teoría del portafolio en el mercado accionario colombiano", *Cuadernos de Economía*, 22(39), Bogotá, 129-168.

Markowitz, H. (1952). "Portfolio Selection". *The Journal of Finance*, 7(1), Mar, 77-91.

Nicholson, W (2007). *Teoría Microeconómica: Principios básicos y ampliaciones*. Novena Edición. Ed. Thomson. México.

Pinilla, R, Valero, L & Guzmán, A. (2007). *Operaciones en el Mercado de Capitales*. Ed. CORREVAL. Tercera Edición. Bogotá Colombia.

Romero, C. (2010). "La teoría moderna de portafolio. Un ensayo sobre sus formulaciones originales y sus repercusiones contemporáneas". *Revista Odeon*, 5 septiembre-enero, 103-118.

Rosillo, J y Martínez, C. (2004). *Modelos de evaluación de Riesgo en decisiones financieras*. Ed. Universidad Externado de Colombia. Bogotá.

Rappaport, A. (1986). *Creating Shareholder Value*. New York. Free Press.

Sheater, S. (2004). "Density Estimation". *Statistical Science* 19(4), 588–597.

Tobin, J. (1958). "Liquidity Preference as Behavior Towards Risk". *The Review of Economic Studies*, 25(2), 65-86.

Villariño, S. (2001). *Turbulencias Financieras y Riesgos de Mercado*. Ed. Prentice Hall. España.

CHAPTER 5

CONSIDERING THE DIRAC DELTA FUNCTION DDF AS AN ANALOGY OF THE BEHAVIOR OF THE COLCAP INDEX 2008-2019

As stated by Tonidandel and Araujo (2015):

Recognized internationally following Paul's work A.M. Dirac (created at the young age of 25 years), one can get an idea of the concept of *impulse* from the old example of the mechanics in which a force concentrated in a short period of time happens at once, for example when a soccer player *kicks* a ball, representing an *impulsive force* applied, to cause a finite change of the linear momentum (of the ball) in an infinitesimal time (p. 3306)[33].

This notion of impulse arises in a field and in a historical moment, in which the questions related to the subatomic roots of matter, contradict the traditional logic of physical thought, with great thinkers like Lord Kelvin, Maxwell himself and Stokes and those had made an emphasis on the development of physics from a purely *mechanistic* position.

In a sense, the scientific debate focused on a struggle between matter/movement, against the further development of *quantum mechanics*, which, to some extent, respected the development of other ideas such as light, heat and electricity and that unleashed the *quantum generation*, which was closer to the constitution of a *mathematical machinery* than to an orthodox fidelity of the mechanistic program. In this context, the quantum theory needed completeness in its approaches, but also a program. Dirac and others knew that quantum theory could not be represented only by common numbers, but that the theory needed complex numbers, which were capable of realizing a new reality shaken by a group of young people under thirty years old. Among other things, the experience of the development of *quantum generation* was the creation of a mathematical arsenal, which included the use of new techniques for the analysis of the physic *micro-phenomenon*. Two excellent works about the development of physics in the first three decades of the past century are the works of Rydnik (1969), Kumar (2011) and Cox & Forshaw (2011). However, Dirac's contributions are not summarized in his contribution to Quantum Mechanics, but to the field of function analysis (if the DDF can be called a function).

In this sense, the DDF can describe these discrete and impulsive behaviors. Unitary functions and especially single scales tend to be a *group* of atypical functions that describe certain behaviors, generally of physical variables across time. One of them is the so-called unitary scalar function USF, or in some cases also called Heaviside's step function (HSF). This function is denoted as $H(x)$, $u(x)$, or in some cases by $\theta(x)$. First, we will analyze some unit scalar functions; later we will explore some characteristics of the delta function to make an analogy with the behavior of the shares in the stock market. Finally, the COLCAP

---

[33] Own translation.

index will be analyzed annually, to make some final considerations in its daily and annual development.

Unitarian Scalar functions

French mathematician Jean D'Alembert (*1717 †1783) believed that the concept of function should be conditional upon the common methods of Algebra and Calculus. However, the great Swiss mathematician Leonhard Euler (*1707 †1783), in turn, had a seemingly simpler view, believing that a function could be defined easily if it were possible. You can draw the curve of $f(t) \times t$, just as you would with a pen by sliding it over a piece of paper.

Frege[34] (1904), - in honor to Boltzmann and with the purpose to define the concept of function -, considers that in recent times, within the very definition of function the word variable has predominated. This, however, needs clarification, considering that any variation occurs over time, therefore, the analysis must be related to the temporal occurrence, since it is the variables that are submitted for consideration. However, what the philosopher perceives is that the analysis does not correlate with time and even in trigonometry, time disappears from any basis of analysis.

Dirac proposes a function that has generally been associated with unit and/or scalar functions, one being Unit Step Function. USF has also been studied by Abramowitz & Stegun (1972) and can be expressed graphically as follows:

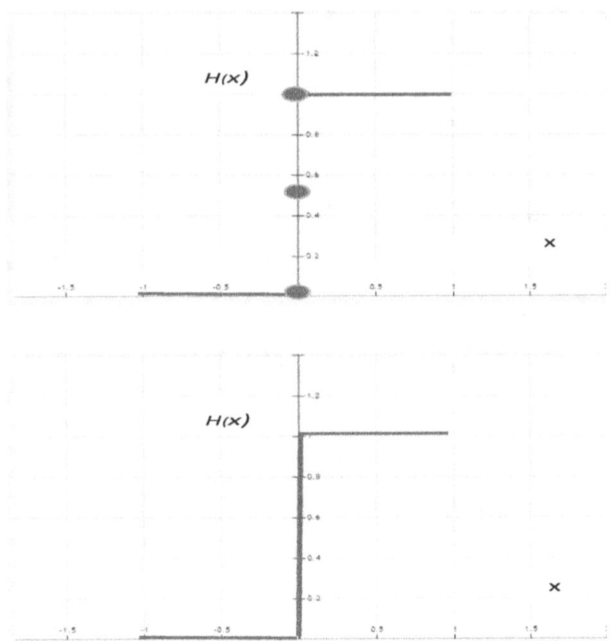

Figure 26 The Unit Step Function an expression graphic. Observe as the function is expressed as signal in (0,0), (0, 0.5) and (0,1). In the second part as a continuous function. Source: Own construction

---

[34] Gottlob Frege (*1848 †1925).

The function goes through -1 to 0 and emits three signals in *(0, 0)* in *(0, 0.5)*, *(0, 1)* and extends to *(1, 1)*. In the second case, there are no opposite signals, but the function is continuous. In this sense, the HSF is defined as a constant piecewise function. This function is represented by:

$$H(x) \begin{cases} 0 & X < 0 \\ \frac{1}{2} & X = 0 \\ 1 & X > 0 \end{cases}$$

(1)

If this is defined as a generalized function $\theta\,(x)$, it can be expressed as:

$$\int \theta(x)\varphi'(x)\,dx = -\varphi(o)$$

(2)

Kanwall (1998) has defined that for $\varphi'(x)$, the derivative is a smooth function that tends to decay very quickly. It is usually used as a notation as follows:

$$Hc(x) \equiv H(x-c)$$

(3)

This function is also associated with the boxcar, sign function and ramp function. It can be either be defined with the function *boxcar* **BC:**

$$\Pi(x) = H\left(x + \frac{1}{2}\right) - H\left(x - \frac{1}{2}\right)$$

(4)

Or it can be defined with the *sign function* **SF:**

$$H(x) = \frac{1}{2}[1 + sgn(x)]$$

(5)

Oppenheim & Wilsky (1983), have studied the relation between the mathematical expression and the signals, or signal function. First, the authors explain the importance of the difference between discrete and continuous measures with relation to time. The discrete-time signal is expressed by *x(n)*, and with the use of brackets [.] (Independent variable). In addition, an interesting example about the behavior of the shares is the COLCAP index, measured daily, where the independent variable (COLCAP Index), is a discrete-time signal used in Colombia for the analysis of the share´s market. Following, we see the COLCAP index in a short period:

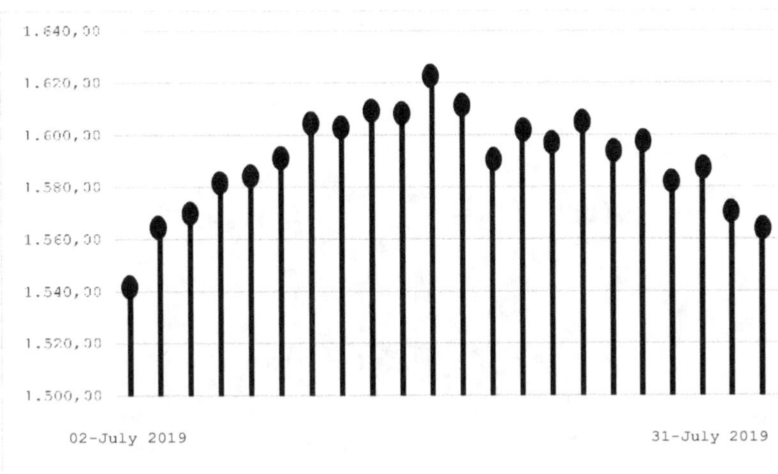

Figure 27 the behavior of the COLCAP Index between 02-July-19 and 31-July 2019. Expressed as a sign. Source: Own construction.

Returning to the function, the derivative of the function is given by:

$$\frac{d}{dx} H(x) = \delta(x) \tag{6}$$

This involves the delta function, which is represented by $\delta(x)$. The function has also been commonly associated with the so-called *ramp function* **RP:**

$$R(x) = xH(x) \tag{7}$$

The derivative is expressed:

$$\frac{d}{dx} R(x) = H(x) \tag{7a}$$

Both functions can be combined in the following function:

$$R(x) = H(x) * H(x) \tag{7b}$$

The expression $H(x)*$ implies a *convolutive* behavior of both functions; the mathematical operator allows the functions to be transformed into another that represents *magnitude* of the superposition of the two initial functions, the second translated and inverted (Hirschman, 1955). Bracewell (2000), regarding the entities of the function considers:

$$H(x) * f(x) = \int_{-\infty}^{x} f(x')dx' \tag{8}$$

If we assume that x is time:

$$H(t) * f(t) = \int_{-\infty}^{\infty} H(u)H(t-u)du \tag{8a}$$

$$= H(0)\int_{0}^{\infty} H(t-u)\,du \tag{8b}$$

$$= H(0)H(t)\int_{0}^{\infty} H(t-u)\,du \tag{8c}$$

If it develops, we have:

$$= H(0)H(t)\int_{0}^{t} H(t-u)\,du \tag{8d}$$

And it results in:

$$= tH(t) \tag{8e}$$

Thus, once the convolution of these functions is resolved, it can be observed in the function if a linear function $ax+b$ is considered:

$$H(ax + b) = H[(x + \tfrac{b}{a})]H(a) + H[-x - \tfrac{b}{a})]H(-a) \tag{9}$$

$$\left[\begin{array}{ll} H\left[x + \dfrac{a}{b}\right] & a > 0 \\[2em] H\left[-x - \dfrac{a}{b}\right] & a < 0 \end{array} \right. \tag{10}$$

The slope of the function on a, and the negative slope on a must be discounted from the negative values of x, as long as a, is less than 0. The USF, in terms of the limits can be defined by:

$$H(x) = \lim\left[\tfrac{1}{2} + \tfrac{1}{\pi} * \tan^{-1}\left(\tfrac{x}{t}\right)\right] \tag{11}$$

So:

$$= \frac{1}{\sqrt{\pi}} \lim_{t \to 0} \int_{-x}^{\infty} t^{-1} e^{-u^2/t^2} \, du \tag{11a}$$

$$= \frac{1}{2} \lim_{t \to 0} \; \operatorname{erfc}\left(\tfrac{-x}{t}\right) \tag{11b}$$

$$= \frac{1}{\pi} \lim_{t \to 0} \int_{-x}^{\infty} t^{-1} \operatorname{sinc}\left(\tfrac{u}{t}\right) du \tag{11c}$$

So that:

$$= \frac{1}{2} + \frac{1}{\pi} \lim_{t \to 0} \sin\left(\tfrac{\pi x}{t}\right) \tag{11d}$$

$$= \lim_{t \to 0} \frac{1}{2} e^{x/t} \quad \text{for } x \le 0 \tag{11e}$$

So that:

$$= \lim_{t \to 0} \frac{1}{2} e^{-x/t} \quad \text{for } x \ge 0 \tag{11f}$$

$$= \lim_{t \to 0} \frac{1}{1 + e^{-x/t}} \tag{11g}$$

$$= \lim_{t \to 0} 1 + e^{-e^{-x/t}} \tag{11h}$$

$$= \frac{1}{2} \lim_{t \to 0} \left[1 + \tanh\left(\tfrac{x}{t}\right)\right] \tag{11i}$$

Finally:

$$= \lim_{t \to 0} \int_{-x}^{\infty} t^{-1} \wedge \left[\frac{x - 1/2t}{t} \right] dx \tag{11j}$$

The ERFC function (complementary error function), states that if *(x)* is the integral sine, *sinec (x)* is the cardinal sine function and $\wedge(x)$ corresponds to the triangular function. As is known, any *monotonic* function that presents horizontal asymptotes that are unequal and constant is a Unitary Scalar Function. If we obtain the *Fourier* transform of this function, we obtain:

$$\mathcal{F}[1 + (x)] = \int_{-x}^{\infty} e^{-2\pi i k x} H(X) dx \tag{12}$$

Below, we have the graphs derived from the *Fourier* transformation:

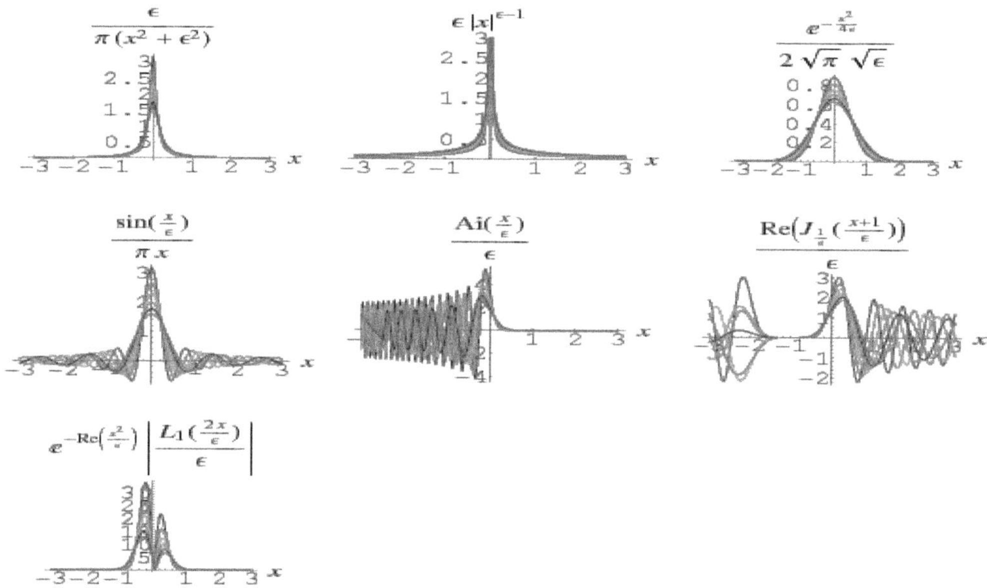

Figure 28 The Fourier transformer in a triangular function and the erfc function. Source: Bracewell (2000).

So that:

$$= \frac{1}{2}[\delta(k) - \frac{i}{\pi k}] \tag{13}$$

Where $\delta(x)$, is the Dirac's Delta Function. Next, we will deepen the Dirac Delta Function.

About de DDF

George & Imaz (1995), state that DDF can have two approaches, one related to mathematics, which considers a distribution and another that, considers it an unusual function that is mainly used in Physics and Engineering. Robinson (1966) has called it a non-standard function and its influence on signal theory is very important (Oppenheim, 1983). The function by Khuri (2004), searched the importance of the relation with the density in terms of non-central moments. In the article written by Chi & Tam (1999), the authors proposed an efficient method to obtain a distribution of a function with one or more random variables applying the DDF in its generalized presentation. The applications of the DDF, can be show in the voltage in circuits with pressing momentary; dampen harmonic oscillator; at point of charge moving in some volume. Some application has relation with the analysis of the density of charge; integration between solutes and solvents and transmission of a pinhole on a dark screen (Mathew & Walker, 1980).

The DDF function is according to Gasiorowicz (1974) a very particular type of function; it must disappear when $x \neq y$, and must be infinite when $x-y = 0$, since the integration range is infinitesimally small. In this way, it is not a function in the usual mathematical sense, but rather a generalized function or a distribution. It does not have a meaning, but it can always be defined in the form:

$$\int dx f(x)\delta(x - a) \tag{14}$$

A function $f(t)$ can be understood simply as a rule that associates a value of t a value of f to each value of t; that is, it is a mapping from t to f symbolized by $f(t): t \rightarrow f(t)$. Therefore, to claim that the DDF is not a function simply because it cannot be hand-drawn is insufficient. In fact, it can be said that the DDF belongs to a more general class of functions, called functional or simply distributions. A functional $\alpha(t)$ can be understood as the process of associating to one arbitrary function $\beta(t)$ and one number $N\alpha[\beta(t)]$:

$$\int_{-\infty}^{\infty} \alpha(t)\beta(dt) = N\alpha[\beta(t)] \tag{14a}$$

The DDF is a generalized function that can be defined as the limit of a delta sequence class (Bracewell, 1999). From the normal point of view, the Delta function is associated with a Schwartz[35] space (S) or the space of all soft functions with compact support D, of the test functions. The delta action in f, is denoted as $\delta[f]$ or is also usually expressed as $< \delta, f >$. This function be a derivation of the unit scalar function:

$$\frac{d}{dx}[H(x)] = \delta(x) \tag{15}$$

---

[35] Laurent Moise Schwartz (*1915 †2002).

The DDF has as its main attribute that the integral of infinity to less infinite is expressed as follow:

$$\int_{-x}^{\infty} f(x)\delta(x-a)dx = f(a) \tag{16}$$

Where it follows:

$$\int_{a+\epsilon}^{a-\epsilon} f(x)\delta(x+a)dx = f(a) \quad \text{For } \epsilon > 0. \tag{16a}$$

Other identities included:

$$\delta(x+a) = 0 \tag{17}$$

For $x \neq a$, so that:

$$\delta(ax) = \frac{1}{|a|}\delta(x) \tag{17a}$$

$$\delta(x^2 - a^2) = \frac{1}{2|a|}[\delta(x+a) + \delta(x-a)] \tag{17b}$$

In general, the DDF of a function x is given by:

$$\delta[g(x)] = \sum_i \frac{\delta(x-x_i)}{|g'(x_i)|} \tag{17c}$$

Where x_i corresponds to the set of the roots of g. Let us look at the following example:

$$\delta(x^2 + x - 2) = \delta[(x-1) + \delta(x+2)] \tag{17d}$$

Hence, $g'(x) = 2x+1$, so that $g'(x_i) = g'(1) = 3$ and $g'(x_2) = g'(-2) = -3$.

So,

$$\delta(x^2 + x - 2) = \frac{1}{3}\delta[(x-1) + \frac{1}{3}\delta(x+2)] \tag{17e}$$

The equation that expresses the derivative of this function is:

$$\int f(x)\delta^{(n)}x\,dx \equiv -\int \frac{\partial f}{\partial x}\delta^{(n-1)}(x)\,dx \qquad (18)$$

If you leave $f(x) = xg(x)$, it results in:

$$\int xg(x)\delta'(x)\,dx = -\int \delta(x)\frac{\partial}{\partial x}[xg(x)] \qquad (18a)$$

So that:

$$= -\int \delta(x)[g(x) + xg'(x)]\,dx \qquad (18b)$$

So:

$$= -\int g(x)\delta(x)\,dx \qquad (18c)$$

In this case, the second term can be deleted to obtain:

$$\int xg'(x)\delta(x)\,dx = 0 \qquad (19)$$

Which involves:

$$x\delta'(x) = -\delta(x) \qquad (19a)$$

If a parallel process is followed, it results in:

$$\int [x^n f(x)]\delta^{(n)}(x)\,dx = (-1)^n \int \frac{\partial^n [x^n f(x)]}{\partial x^n}\delta(x)\,dx \qquad (20)$$

After Dirac, introduces the Bra and Ket vectors, in his Principles of Quantum Mechanics (1930), he refers to the DDF, as a function that satisfies the following conditions:

$$\int_{-x}^{\infty} \delta(x)\,dx = 1 \qquad (21)$$

Moreover, it will present a different behavior for

$$\delta(x) = 0 \qquad\qquad (21a)$$

If you want to have an image of the function, you must consider a function of the real variable x that is null and that is outside a domain of amplitude ε around the origin $x = 0$ and that the inside of that domain is equal a 1. The exact form of the function internally does not matter if it does not have unnecessarily strong variations (for example if the function is of order ε^{-1}). Going to the limit for $\varepsilon \to 0$, the function will tend to be confused with $\delta(x)$.

$\delta(x)$ is not a function of x according to the traditional definition of function, since the definition would require having a defined value for each point in the domain. It is what I would like to define as an improper function, which highlights fundamental differences with ordinary functions. In this way, the DDF is a function that can allow within the mathematical analysis with the same comfort as that of the other functions, as long as non-logical consequences are generated.

The Economic Time

On the other hand, just as Frege (1907), introduced the notion of time in relation to the concept of function, there is a difference between *physical time, economic time* and *psychological time*. In principle, we can recognize that physical time is a space of analysis very different from that posed by other disciplines. Uttal (2008) has made an analysis of *physical* and *psychological* time, recognizing that the *physical phenomenon* has a certain criterion of affinity with the *psychological phenomenon*. For example, in physics, the instruments of observation of the minuscule have not allowed us to approach the internal reality of the atom and elementary particles much more direct manner.

However, the mathematical arsenal of quantum mechanics provides a favorable and in-depth theoretical analysis of the reality of the particles. In this way, -the author insists-, there is a contradiction between behavioral currents, mainly of cognitive mentalism, which based on the question: what happens in the mind?, and the question: what happens with the behavior of elementary particles?, try to build a field of similar analysis that provides an explanatory theoretical *corpus* but with a limitation, in contrast to the observed reality.

However, to explain this space, that of the very small, different theorists have turned to analog models that try to account for the internal constitution of matter. Bohr[36] himself used a *heliocentric* model, with a paradigmatic idea, that gave light to the so-called quantum leap. Although, some locate the origin of quantum mechanics in the study of black body radiation, studied by Planck and which resulted in its famous constant, is not the concept of quantum leap, a fundamental pillar in such development. Why is it that the changes introduced by quantum theory are comparable to those that the *cognitive* revolution brings in the psychological field?

---

[36] Niels Henrik David Bohr (*1885 †1962).

Whatever the arguments for or against this comparison, it is very likely that the further development of physical science qualitatively demonstrates the hypotheses made by the physics of the twentieth century and the psychology that emerges as the basis of the associated ways of thinking the so-called cognitive mentalism. In this context the analysis of time comes from a Greek tradition that can be traced from *Anaximander* in the differentiation between *apeiron* (τὸ ἄπειρον), and *arche (ἀρχή)*, that is, the unlimited and the infinite. Time is the indefinitely extensive and that in contrast to the conformation of the *cosmos*; it had neither beginning nor end. Other thinkers as *Melissus of Samos*, -follower of Parmenides-, denied the future and considered that what exists is *apeiron* has neither beginning nor end. That concept is extended even to space - the unlimited applies to extension and duration. The delimitation of the unlimited, through the imposition of the number, which provides regularity, proportion, and measure, gives a character of geometric proportion of the extension, which is consolidate in the different forms that matter acquires. Time, on the other hand, is directly relate to the movements of the stars and the celestial bodies that provide a measure to it through the daily, nocturnal, monthly, and annual cycles. Time ceases to be a succession to constitute a measurable element. In *Timaeus* (Τίμαιος), Plato argues that time is the result of a divine creation and in a later phase the being is located (an ideal model of the cosmos in the future), the becoming (which obeys the disorganized matter) and space, which therefore does not leave a mythical vision of divine creation of time. Aristotle, on the other hand, introduces the idea of before and after the number of the movement with respect to the before and after, is what for the *stagirite*, represents time, which can only exist if there are conscious beings capable of performing the action of enumerate.

We generally conceive the idea of a clock, which serves to measure time, but the *Platonic-Aristotelian* idea is itself a kind of clock, a criterion for the measurement of time. Time is then the movement or the measure of movement in its regularity and constancy. On the other hand, Aristotle considered that time was the sphere of everything, because everything happens in time, in the surrounding sphere (Guthrie, 1964).

Without a doubt the version of time from a physical posture, could be summed up in the idea of its symbiotic union with space. *Space-time* implies a different vision of the traditional perception of time in classical mechanics. A schematic posture no longer persists, and the rupture of that traditional vision cannot be analyzed without recognizing the influence of physical thought of the early twentieth century. In relation to *economic time*, Zumbach (1997) performs an interesting analysis of the difference between *physical time* and *economic time*. Based on the classic definitions establishes some time scales for the use of financial phenomena.

For the author, the scales are:

Business Time	Transaction time 1	Transaction time 2	Theta-time (θ)	Tau-time (τ)
Counts only when a given market is open, chopping off nights and-weekends. It is the most used.	Add one for each transaction.	Add the value of each transaction.	Add a measure of the seasonal volatility. Contract or expand of the physical time.	Add some measure of the momentary recent volatility. Contract or expand of the physical time.

Table 26 Classification of the time in Economics. Source: Own construction based on Zumbach (1997)

Behavior of the shares (Heaviside and Delta)

For the behavior of a share or one set of shares, a situation such as the following:

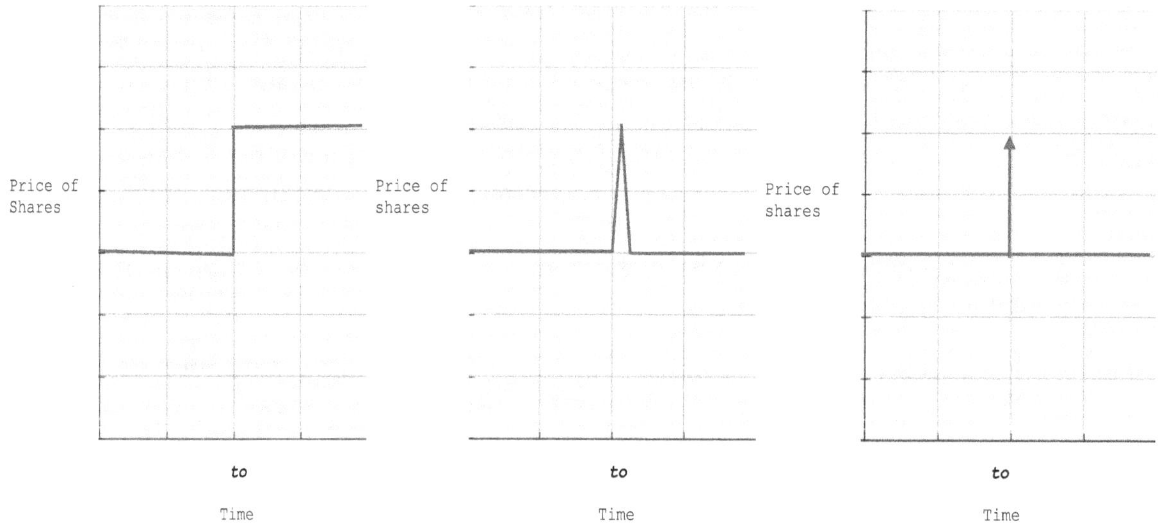

Figure 29 Probability of the behavior of the shares in the short time. Analogical as an impulse event. Source: Own Construction.

We assume that a stock has a constant market price over time and at one point, there is a significant increase that is again sustained over a relatively short period. These increases may be due to external shocks or endogenous situations of listed companies (purchase of assets, incorporation of new technologies, innovation, trust, oligopolistic movements, increase in profits, etc.). In this sense, the function that best describes the behavior of the share (whether common or preferred), is the unit scalar function specially the HSF.

However, a share - unlike the case of a behavior similar to that of the unit scalar function - may present a significant increase in its value, and over time, return to its initial state. Generally, the behavior of these shares can be associated with a unit *impulse function*, which, like the scalar function, is rare in its practical applications. In addition, similar behavior can be evidenced in short periods of variation in the price of the shares. Dirac's function can be overlapped to a stock impulse event, which can be interpreted as follows (Butkov, 1968; Moore, 1990). If the DDF is expressed as:

$$\delta(x) = \begin{cases} \infty & x = 0 \\ \\ 0 & x \neq 0 \end{cases}$$

$$(22)$$

So that $\forall a, b \in \mathbb{R}\ a<0<b$:

$$\int_a^b \delta(x)\,dx = 1 \tag{23}$$

Be f: $\mathbb{R}\_\mathbb{R}$ a continuous function, we have:

$$\int_a^b \delta(x)f(x)\,dx = f(0), \forall a,b \in \mathbb{R}\ a < 0 < b \tag{24}$$

If we consider an increase in the stock market price at a given time, which we will call p_1 at a time t_n and we have a base value of the p_0 share, we can find the following situation:

$$\delta(t) = \begin{cases} p_1 \rightarrow \infty & x = t_n \\ \\ p_0 & x \neq t_n \end{cases}$$

$$(25)$$

Suppose now the integral between two periods' t_1 and t_2. Assumes that this integral is equal to 1, as proposed in the development of the DDF function:

$$\int_{t1}^{t2} \delta(x)\,dx = 1 \tag{26}$$

If we evaluate the integral for a value a and b and find an *impulse event* in c that increases the price up to 1/2 *(t)*, we will have to:

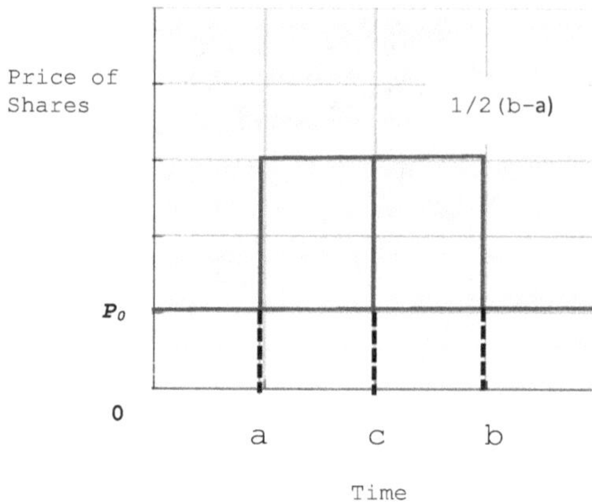

Figure 30 Integral for a value a and b and an impulse event. Source: Own Construction.

The extrapolation of these ideas implies changes with respect to the DDF, in relation to the case of the shares. It is based on a base price, which does not necessarily imply that it is located at $x = 0$. On the other hand, the impulse is given in discrete periods of time and the *impulse event* does not happen at $y = 0$. However, the analogy allows analyzing the behavior of the share, its market price in three instant moments. Hence:

$$d(b\text{-}a)t = \begin{cases} \tfrac{1}{2}(b\text{-}a) & a < c < b \\ \\ p_o & \text{in other values.} \end{cases} \tag{27}$$

If we assume that $b\text{-}a=2$, we will have to meet that:

$$\int_{t1}^{t2} \delta(t)\,dt = 2(b-a) * \frac{1}{2(b-a)} = 1 \tag{28}$$

So that:

$$= \int_a^b \frac{1}{2(b-a)} = \left(\frac{t}{2}\right)(b-a)\Big[_a^b \tag{29}$$

$$= \frac{(b-a)}{2(b-a)} + \frac{(b-a)}{2(b-a)} = \frac{(b-a)+(b-a)}{2(b-a)} = 1 \tag{29a}$$

To derive the DDF, we need to define it in an interval *(a-β, a+β)*, which joins with a linear stroke:

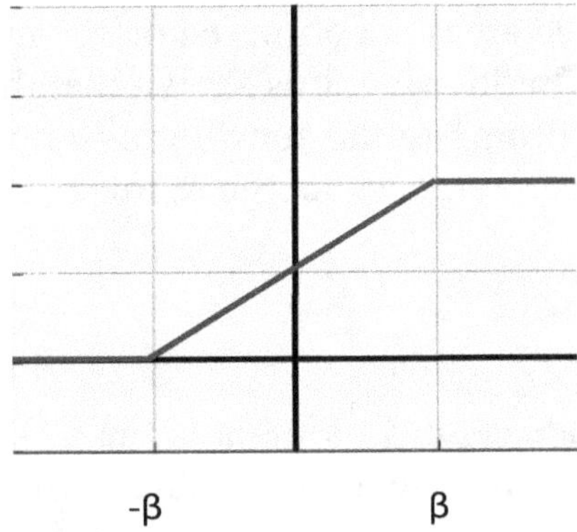

Figure 31. Derivate form the DDF with an interval (a-β, a+β). Source: Own Construction.

The derivative of the function will present two jumps and it has an enormous utility in Physics and Engineering. We considered the $\delta(x)$ function with two linear traces. So, the graphic expression is as follows:

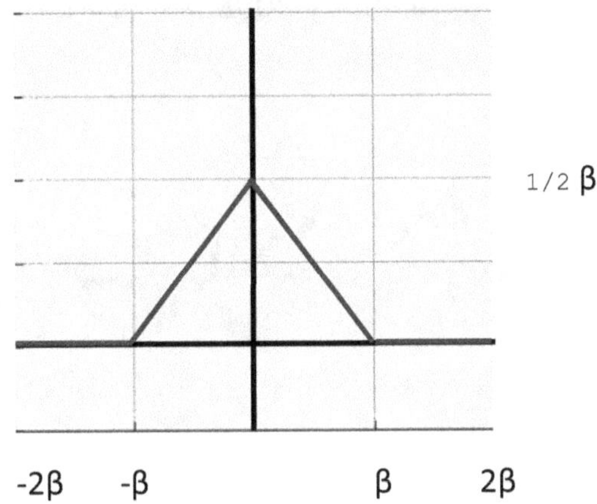

Figure 32 Jumps in the derivate form the DDF. Source: Own Construction.

In the process of derivation $\delta'(x)$, we obtain:

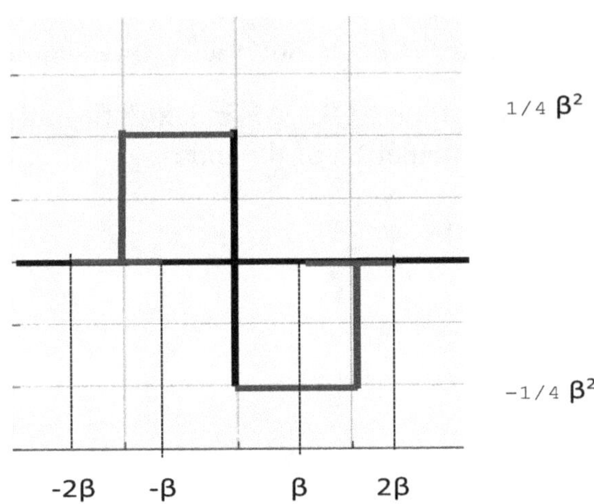

Figure 33 The derivate form of the DDF. Source: Own Construction.

In this process, two well-defined areas are observed on the negative and positive side of the plane that have the same area. In this way, it is shown that the function has a jump or jump in β and another in -β and according to the substitution rule, it has two linear strokes. For calculations related to the *nth* derivate see George & Imaz (1997).

The COLCAP Index

One of the most recognized indexes in Colombia is the COLCAP index, corresponding to the calculation and registration of twenty (20) shares of liquid that are traded on the Colombian BVC Stock Exchange. In the index, the market capitalization value determines the weighting to participate in it. The index started on January 15th, 2008 and is a base index of 1,000 points. In the event of the disappearance of share registered in the COLCAP basket, a rebalancing process must be carried out, with a maximum per company of 20% of the total basket. If this limit is exceeded, the rebalancing procedure must be carried out and the surplus will be distributed among the other participants. Below we observe the behavior of the COLCAP index, over the period January 2008, August 2019.

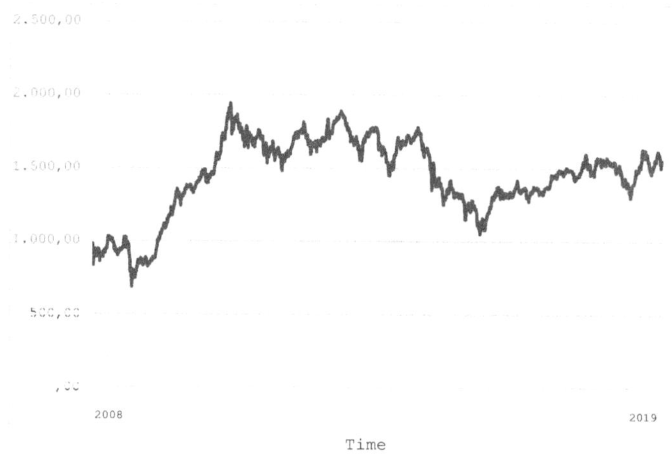

Figure 34 The behavior of the COLCAP Index 2008-2019. Source: Own construction based on BVC data.

The appendix shows the behavior of the COLCAP index until mid-August of this year. The following equation expresses the calculation of the index:

$$I^k(t) = E \sum_{i=1}^{n} w_i^k \ Pi(t) \tag{30}$$

Where:

$I^k(t)$ = Index value for the period *(t)*.

(t) = Day or instant at which the index is calculated.

k = Term of validity of the COP or weighting for share *i*, fixed for *k*.

E = factor that allows continuity to the index if there is rebalance of the basket or corporate adjustments.

n = number of shares in the index at the time *(t)*.

P = Current closing price of the share *i* in *t*.

w_i^k = Weight or weighting for share *i*, fixed during *k*.

For the COLCAP basket, the shares must meet the following requirements:

Requirement.	Description.
Cash operation.	It refers to the fact that in the period of 90 calendar days prior to the date of selection of the basket, there is at least one cash transaction
Registration of the share.	The share must be registered 30 calendar days before the effective date of the basket.
Active Condition of the share.	The status of the share must be *Active*, that is, that the share has presented an official quotation during the last 30 calendar days and / or that it presents offers in force in the trading system.
Shares that generate dividends.	Registered shares must generate dividends
Colombian Global Market.	The group of foreign securities issued outside the country by national or foreign issuers will not be considered in the COLCAP selection process.
Annual re-composition of the basket.	This review will include and exclude actions that meet or not meet the necessary requirements; the baskets will be valid for one year. In the re-composition process, the participation in the *index* of each selected stock for the following quarter is determined. COLCAP will be recomposed after the market closes on the last business day of October and will be effective between the first business day of November of the same year and the last business day of October of the following year.
Quarterly Weighting.	The index basket is recomposed annually. The weighting of the basket will be recalculated quarterly with rebalancing. Each share within the index basket varies daily according to the behavior of the prices of the same in the secondary market. Thus, to avoid excessive participation of an issuer for extended periods, the BVC rebalances the index basket quarterly. The rebalancing of COLCAP will take place on the last business day of the months of January, April, and July of each year.

Table 27 Requirements of the COLCAP Index. Source: Own construction based on BVC

The different behaviors that shares can adopt are reflected in the behavior of the COLCAP index. Thus, when observing some specific years, the significant changes that can be evidenced result in the expression of *impulse events,* which for the specific case of the Colombian index we could group into:

i) Rebalancing: as explained in principle, this change corresponds to a process of calibration of the intervening shares, which, as shown in the before table, allows the most important shares of the Colombian stock market to be located therein. *Impulse events* are in this case endogenous event.

ii) Changes in the price of underlying assets: this case refers to changes in the market price of the assets that are related to the companies in their sectorial location. In the Colombian case, some shares have had strong shocks, generally due to the international prices of the products offered. These *impulse events* are generally exogenous and tend to behave randomly in the short term, but aspects related to the economic cycle can also be evidenced (Hull, 2017).

iii) Randomity of the *impulse events*: these may arise specifically from the fact that the shares are traded in a free competition market and that their market price is subject to the daily movement in the stock quote wheel and that may be affected by the economic agents that can act through expectations, not always in a rational way. This is an intrinsic and endogenous aspect of the process itself, in the logic of the stock market. Analyzes made from the observation of the random walk and the Brownian motion are relevant aspects of the relationship between economics and physics that have formally accounted for this aspect (Sinha *et. al,* 2001).

iv) Rational consumer behavior: in this case, the individual who buys shares in the stock market will, in principle, seek to satisfy the axiom of profit maximization and cost minimization. However, this behavior is only considered as attached to the consumer and is not considered extensive to the corporations and listed companies (criticisms of this approach can be seen in Tversky & Kahneman, (1974, 1979, and 1981). On the other hand, the influence that may have on the consumer, buying trends that generate momentum events should not be dismissed. X, can act irrationally, buying shares a, without a duly justified cause and this share will generate a chain reaction and in a sense a *wagon effect* in the stock market.

Methodology

First, we obtain the *standard deviation* per year form the data of COLCAP index. The next step is analyzing the situation of the behavior of the index in periods of reference. For example, we have four years with wide dispersion. Nevertheless, the different functions studied, must show a similar behavior as the DDF, maybe the behavior is very similar, but is important to recognize, that the analogy purpose is the result of the observation in different graphics. However, the demonstration is related to the impulse function or DDF. In the years observed, seven have a positive *slope* in the behavior of the index. We can perceive a relative improvement in the understanding of the importance of deepening of the stock market. Then, we analyze the specific moments of possible impulse events in the years of greatest dispersion.

Results

In different years, impulse moments affected by various processes are observed. However, these processes happen in a limited time and measured discreetly, usually in daily periods. The behavior of the index shows significant variations in the years 2009, 2010, 2014 and 2015, while in the other years, there are less dispersed behaviors. Then, it can be deduced that in these years referenced in principle, there is a greater probability of occurrence of impulse events than in the other years. This postulate can generate debate; however, we will concentrate on these four years, to evaluate the influence of impulse events in the index and determine the existence or not of similar behaviors.

The next table shows the standard deviation:

Year	Standard Deviation
2008	75.36319
2009	**187.4582**
2010	**182.3206**
2011	71.36613
2012	60.91
2013	81.72
2014	**91.26476**
2015	**92.02925**
2016	68.59593
2017	56.1457
2018	65.88096
2019	68.23215

Table 28 Standard deviation. Source: Own construction.

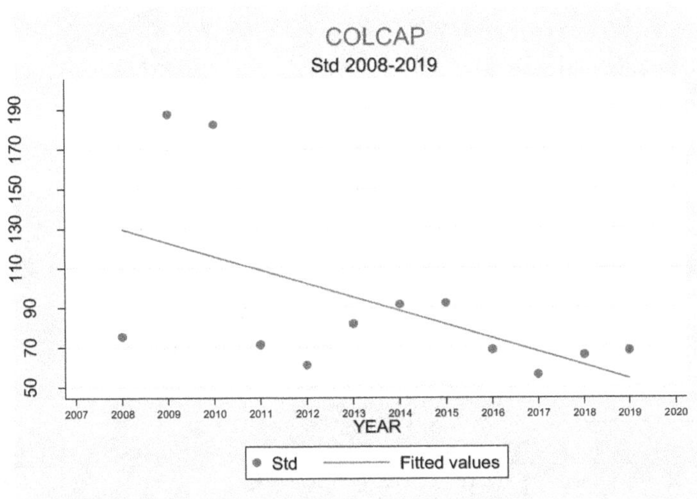

Figure 35 Standard deviation COLCAP index 2008-2019. Source: Own construction based on BVC.

For the year 2009, an index behavior is found, which can be seen in the following figure in the months of August and in the month of December. In August, the days 27th, 28th and 31st are observed with an index value of 1210.09, 1214.38 and 1209.09, respectively. For the month of December, the behavior of the actions of days 23rd, 24th and 28th has been taken. The values are 1364.13, 1372.72 and 1365.06.

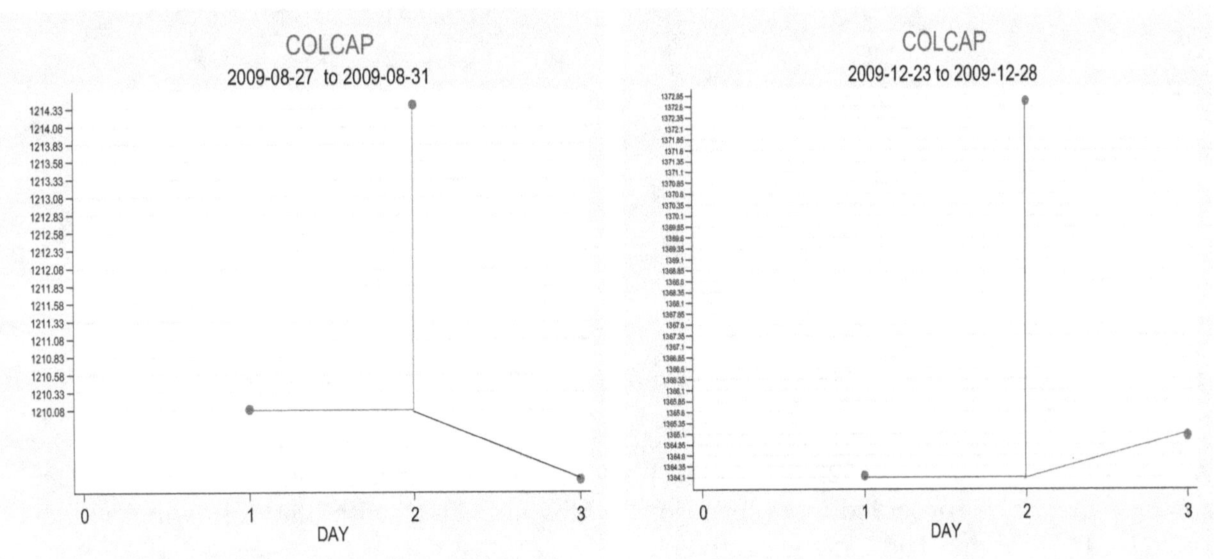

Figure 36 Behavior of COLCAP index 2009. Source: Own construction based on BVC.

For the year 2010, we have as reference dates from January 18 to January 20th. The values for these days are 1382.07, 1386.01 and 1381.80, respectively. In this same year, another change is observed between February 1st and 3rd, with the following values 1358.49, 1363.85 and 1359.43. Finally, there is a significant change between March 24th and 26th with the following values, respectively.

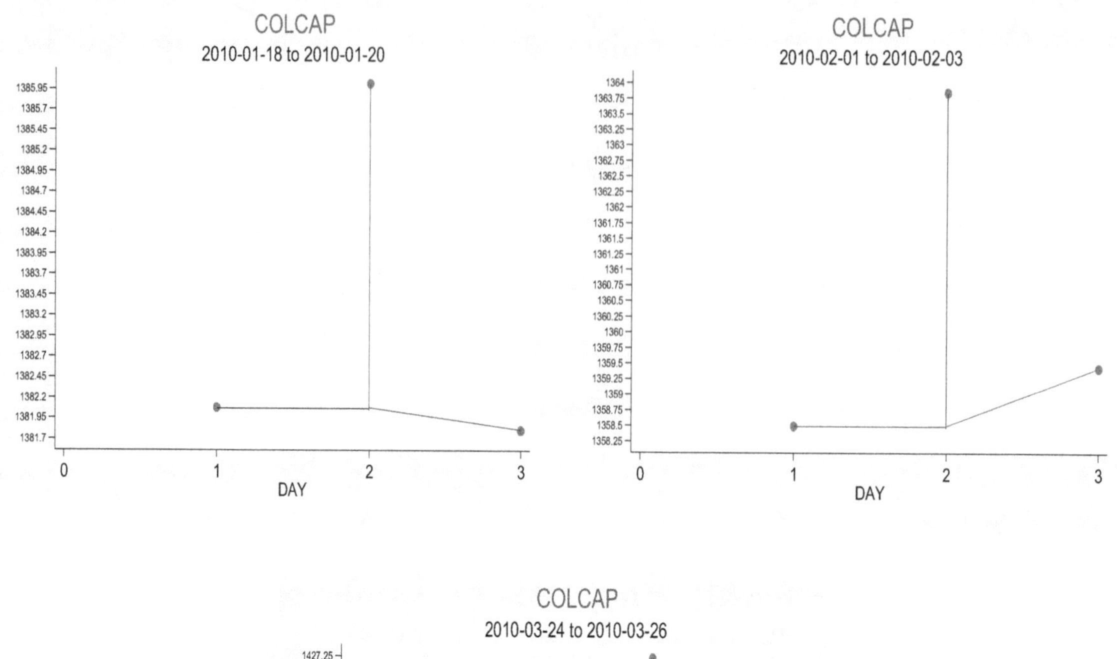

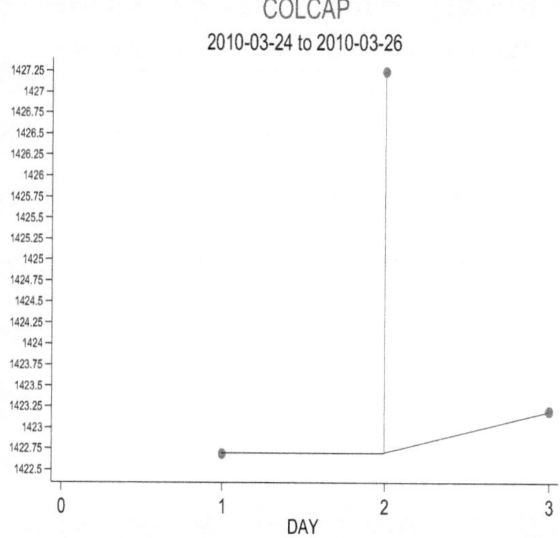

Figure 37 Behavior of COLCAP index 2010. Source: Own construction based on BVC.

For the year 2014, we have as reference dates from February 21st to February 25th. The values for these days are 1520.60, 1535.11 and 1501.40, respectively. In this same year, another change is observed between April 15th and 21st, with the following values 1669.24, 1677.73 and 1668.85, respectively.

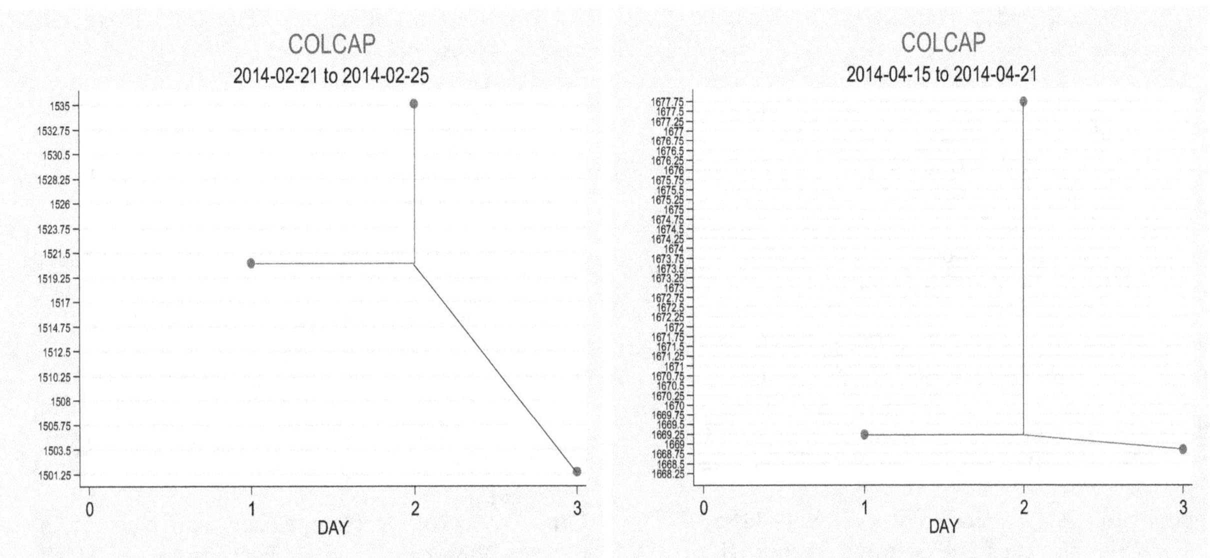

Figure 38 Behavior of COLCAP index 2014. Source: Own construction based on BVC.

References

Au, C & Tam, J. (1999). Transforming variables using the Dirac Generalized Function. The American Statistician, 53:3, pp. 270-272.

Abramowitz, M and Stegun, I. (1972). Handbook of Mathematical Functions with Formulas, graphs, and Mathematical Tables. National Bureau of Standards Applied Mathematics Series 55.

Bracewell, R. (2000). "Heaviside´s Unit Step Function, H(x)". The Fourier Transform its applications, 3rd ed. New York: Mc Graw Hill, pp. 61-65.

Butkov, E. (1968). Mathematical Physics. Addison-Wesley Publishing Company, Inc. Cop.

Cox, B & Forshaw, J. (2011) The Quantum Universe: Everything that can Happen Does Happen. Penguin Random House.

Dirac, P, M. (1958). The Principles of Quantum Mechanics, Oxford University Press, Cambridge, 1958, 4ª ed.

Dirac, P.M. (2012). Lectures on Quantum Mechanics and Relativistic Field Theory. Notes by K. K. Gupta and George Sudershan. Martino Publishing Mansfield Centre, CT. New York.

Frege, G. (1904). ¿Qué es una función? En G. Frege, Ensayos de semántica y filosofía de la lógica. Traducción. Luis Manuel Valdés, Madrid: Tecnos.

Gasiorowicz, S. (1974). Quantum Physics, John Wiley and Sons, Inc., New York.

Guthrie, W. (1962). A History of Greek Philosophy. Volume I. The earlier pre-Socratic and the Pythagoreans. Cambridge University Press.

George, K. & Imaz, C. (1995). La Delta de Dirac como Función. Educación matemática Vol 7. N° 3. Diciembre, pp. 48-57.

Hirschman, I, I. and Widder, D, V. (1955). The Convolution transforms. Princeton University Press.

Hull, J. (2017). Options, Futures and Other Derivatives. Ninth Edition. Pearson.

Kanwall, R, P. (1998). Generalized Functions: Theory and Technique, 2nd Edition. Boston, MA: Birkhauser.

Khuri, A. (2004). Applications of Dirac´s delta function in statistics. International Journal of Mathematical Education in

Science and Technology. Vol 35:2, pp. 185-195.

Kumar, M. (2011). QUANTUM: Einstein, Bohr, and the Great Debate about the Nature of Reality. WW Norton & Co.

Mantegna, Rosario, N. & Stanley, H. Eugene. (2000). An Introduction to Econophysics. Cambridge University Press.

Mathew, J and Walker, R. (1980). Methods of mathematical physics. Wiley-Estern.

Moore, E, N. (1990). Theoretical Mechanics. Krieger Publishing Company. November.

Oppenheim, A. V. and Wilsky, A.S. (1983). Signals and Systems. Prentice-Hall International, Inc.

Tonidandel, D, A, V. and Araujo, A, E, A. The delta function revisited: from Heaviside to Dirac. *Rev. Bras. Ensino Fís.* 2015. Vol.37, N° 3, pp. 3306-1-3306-9. http://dx.doi.org/10.1590/S1806-11173731851.

Rydnik, V. (1969). Qu´est-ce que la mécanique quintique?. Éditions de Moscou.

Robinson, A. (1974). Non-Standard Analysis, North-Holland Publishing Co. Amsterdam, 1966, Rev, ed.

Sinha, S. Chatterjee, A. Chakraborti, A & Chakraborti, B. (2011). Econophysics.

An Introduction. Physics Textbook. Wiley-VCH.

Tversky, A. y Kahneman, D. (1974). Judgement Under Uncertainty: Heuristic and Biases. Science (Nez Series), 185(4157), pp. 1124-1131.

Tversky, A. y Kahneman, D. (1979). Prospect Theory: An Analysis of Decision under Risk. Econometrica, 47(2), pp. 263-292.

Tversky, A. y Kahenman, D. (1981). The Framing of Decisions and the Psychology of Choice. Science (New Series), 211(4481), pp. 453-458.

Uttal, W. (2008). Time, Space, and Number in Physics and Psychology. Sloan Publishing, New York.

Vera Ramirez, H. (2019). The application of Determinants to the relationship between productive factors: underproduction and preliminaries of Dirac. La tecnología al servicio de la educación objetivos de desarrollo sostenible. Colombia ISBN 978-958-59982-6-1 Ed: Teinco, 2019, pp.17 – 47.

Zumbach, G. (1997). Considering time as the random variable: a new point of view for studying financial time series. Econophysics: An Emergent Science. Proceedings of the 1st Workshop on Econophysics, Editors: K. Kertész, I, Kondor.   Budapest

EPILOGUE

The theoretical review on the subject of innovation, offers a set of theories that focus on aspects related to entrepreneurship, the advance in investment in innovation and the consolidation of politics in Latin American countries, focused on achieving better levels of incorporation of this investment, mainly in the small productive units. However, it is found that the countries of the zone are lagging in relation to the need to influence in a decisive way these aspects that are related to the few resources allocated to research and development. Thus, as held by the IDB (2010) for Latin American countries:

> One characteristic is the low level of expenditure and intensity in R & D ... On average, the intensity of R & D in companies (as a percentage of sales) is less than 0.2%, much lower than the averages of 0, 61 of Europe or 1.89 of the OECD (IDB, 2010, p.19)[37].

On the other hand, the construction of internal indexes tied to elements within the firms or productive units can contribute to their internal development and to monitor the proposed actions to incorporate elements related to investment in innovation. Finally, the model does not suggest an important and strong relationship between the export of goods with high technology and the GDP per capita GDP, but a significant relationship with foreign direct investment, which suggests that investment in innovation will depend much more of money flows that manage to enter inter -countries and that focus on this area. For this, without a doubt, a clear policy on the part of the states is needed to provide legal support for the action from the micro business to the large corporations.

Based on Carvajal's (2002) proposals, the construction of a model proposal was carried out that included everything from iconic elements to mathematical elements, making an important emphasis on three fundamental points: the sources of investment, the productive factors and the incorporation of technology and equipment. In principle, it was observed how historically a transit was carried out that went from the family business to the small and medium business. This transit can still be associated with elements that permeate many internal behaviors of MSMEs, in relation to their internal organization, since they continue to function more as families than actually as productive units do. Based on the analysis of elements derived mainly from microeconomics, it has been possible to develop a proposal that focuses on the importance of productive factors, taking into account also the need for productive units to incorporate technology that achieves in some way generate surpluses that allow, through the passage to economies of scale and abandoning the stage of productive adolescence, seek to enter the macro system of large corporations and the attempt to generate surpluses to export indirectly or directly. Although Latin American

---

[37] Own translation.

dynamics indicate that small and medium enterprises have focused from the state economic policies to become a development space, it is important to generate support strategies that allow them to access credit and incorporate technical elements that have therefore productive improvement and the follow-up to it.

Productive factors such as capital and labor are still basic to be able to generate substantial improvements in their replacement rate, as well as variables related to investment, equipment and technology.

The interdisciplinary relations between Economics and Physics give us an important index in the works of Paul Adrian Maurice Dirac. His equations, solved brilliantly by the physicist, have similarities with some production functions and it could be asserted that the solution found by Dirac can contribute to the analysis of the relationship of productive factors: capital and labor. The example used, explains an advantage position occupied for the United States and Japan with respect to other countries. However, we see an important value of the determinant in Canada and Finland. Unfortunately, countries as Tanzania, Peru, Mexico and Kenya have a determinant with a value less than 0. The ranking with respect to the quantitative measure about the relation between productive factors show a better level in countries with high-income vs countries with low-income levels. The determinant will be an opportunity for research about the choice over the factor most important in every country.

On other hand the study of the interactions between factors, but can also become a mechanism of interdisciplinary relationship between physics and economics, leaving aside the traditional relationship between both disciplines, which has focused mainly on the stochastic analysis of prices, its relationship with the movement Brownian and the discrete and complex analysis. On the other hand, it is an analogical way of evidencing interactions between models from both sciences, with the aim of contributing to economic development, without neglecting the essential foundations of economic science, in terms of the traditionally accepted and studied functions of production. If we look at recent financial movements, we can find that physics contributes to explain financial imbalances or catastrophes.

According to Stanley, Amaral, Gabaix, Gopikrishnana & Pleroua (2001):

> We shall see that our analysis of empirical data shows that those catastrophic rare events are a part of the overall picture—that they are not simply inexplicable disasters beyond any possible understanding. Although this sounds as though we physicists think we can contribute to economics, it is possible that the converse will turn out to be even truer. If we join economists in studying economics, we may stumble onto some ideas that will help us back in our more traditional research areas of physics. An example is turbulence. If I stir a bucket of water, energy is added to

the system on a big scale. This energy then dissipates over progressively smaller scales. This is an unsolved physics problem; many empirical facts can be stated, but little can be said about understanding it. (Stanley, Amaral, Gabaix, Gopikrishnana & Pleroua, 2001, p. 4).

In the stud of the theory of Portfolio, we find a negative covariance in the relationship between ECOPETROL and PACIFIC, and positive between PAZ DEL RIO and PACIFIC and between PAZ DEL RIO and ECOPETROL. In principle, a portfolio that privileges a larger basket among these PEACE OF THE RIO AND PACIFIC shares would be considered much more recommendable for the investor, but that contradictorily presents inverse relations with negative slopes in their functions and low levels of association. The relationship between ECOPETROL and PAZ DEL RIO presents a positive covariance, with linear functions that show positive slopes as well. This combination of shares would be much more desirable despite having a lower covariance than the previous combination, but with positive slopes. Finally, it is important to note that the combination of these three companies, in a multiple regression function, in which ECOPETROL share prices are considered as dependent on the share price of the other two companies, shows the following results:

A constant of the share price of ECOPETROL of COP 914.8207, a coefficient for PACIFIC of COP -0.1214162 and for PAZ DEL RIO of COP 65, 28836, with a low *r adjusted* equivalent to COP 0.2929[38]. The model can be expressed as follows:

$$(10)\ y_i = 914{,}8207 + 65{,}28836X_1 - 0{,}1214162X_2 + v_i$$

The TP continues to have a significant importance in the orientation of the investor in terms of the weighting of a portfolio basket, regardless of whether it refers to fixed income or variable income. The evidence found in this article is only due to a basket of equities of three (3) companies listed on the stock exchange in Colombia in 2016 and it finds that for the investor should focus on those actions that present: higher levels of correlation,

---

[38] Here is how the model can be formalized:

yi = α + 1X1 + 2X2 + vi [1]

Conventions:

yi = Value of the shares of ECOPETROL.
α = Value of the shares of ECOPETROL, independent of variations in the shares of PACIFIC and PAZ DEL RIO.
X1 = Price of the shares of PAZ DEL RIO.
X2 = Price of the shares of PACIFIC.
β1 = Value β Coefficient of variation between PAZ DEL RIO and ECOPETROL.
β2 = Value β Coefficient of variation between PACIFIC and ECOPETROL.
υi = Random error of the regression.

relationship between covariance of the prices of both shares and pending of the linear functions that relate the prices of the shares in dual relationships.

In the Delta function is possible to analyze the behavior of the shares of different companies participating in the stock market, through different quantitative tools and methods that can be provided by other disciplines or sources, such as physics. Although, the relationship between Economics and Physics is the relationship between a discipline daughter of modernity and another born in Greek antiquity, it allows, however, a fruitful dialogue and the exchange of analytical instruments (Vera, 2018). The measurement of a stock index such as COLCAP, in its discrete expression, can be analyzed from the analogy as a variable very similar to the variables studied in physics in *impulse events*. An impulse event, analyzed as a discrete variable over time, allows the daily change of the share to be seen as an expression of this impulse. In most cases and from a vocation that we could call *macro time series analysis*, there is a description more consistent with the idea of a continuous variable, expressed by a certain function. However, unlike many physical variables, whose behavior, far from being random, moves through certain patterns in which, the actions in the stock market, can have and in fact they have behaviors of excessive dispersion.

APPENDIX A

BRIEF MODEL OF EXPORTS OF HIGH-TECH PRODUCTS.

In order to analyze the importance of investment, in principle, a model was run that tries to associate innovation as an element related to the improvement in the production of goods that imply the incorporation of high technology, -this variable is expressed as a dollar value over the total exports of each country analyzed-, against two fundamental variables that are: foreign direct investment in its net flow and the internal product per capita, expressed in dollars. The time taken is the period 2000-2015, for thirteen (13) countries.

The model can be expressed as follows:

$$HT = \beta_0 + \beta_1 FI + \beta_2 GDP_{PC} + U_t$$

Where:

HT= Exports of high-tech products.

FI = Foreign direct investment (net flow).

GDP_{pc} = Gross Domestic Product (per capita).

U_t = Error.

The results found in the model, using STATA as the base software, suggest the following elements. A relatively low adjustment factor, which implies that the association between the variable HT and the vraiables GDP per capita and FDI, is only 41.9%. The model presents a low level of adjustment. Despite this, the coefficients for each of the cases suggest a model that is expressed as follows:

$$HT = 814000000 + 0{,}0000099 FDI - 37460{,}3 GDPpc$$

Exports of high-technology products show negative results for the case of the gross and secondary domestic product, but very low for extra-heavy direct investment, which means that the increase in the level of exports of this type of products is not directly related to better levels or significant increases in the gross domestic product per capita and per capita, but in a smaller proportion to the level of foreign direct investment flows. However, it is important to recognize that the level of ause of the model is low, which suggests the intervention of other variables in the relationship with the percentage of exported goods with high technological value.

In the following table, we find the data obtained for the referenced time period:

Source	SS	df	MS
Model	5.8861e+17	2	2.9431e+17
Residual	5.5202e+17	10	5.5202e+16
Total	1.1406e+18	12	9.5053e+16

Number of obs	=		13
F(2, 10)	=		5.33
Prob > F	=		0.0265
R-squared	=		0.5160
Adj R-squared	=		0.4192
Root MSE	=		2.3e+08

High_techn~s	Coef.	Std. Err.	t	P>|t|	[95% Conf. Interval]	
Foreign_Di~t	9.92e-07	3.16e-07	3.14	0.011	2.88e-07	1.70e-06
GDP_Per_ca~a	-37460.3	25302.48	-1.48	0.170	-93837.74	18917.13
_cons	8.14e+08	1.68e+08	4.84	0.001	4.39e+08	1.19e+09

Below are the values estimated through two partial regressions that establish the relationship between exports of high-technology products vs. foreign direct investment and exports of high-technology products vs. per capita gross domestic product.

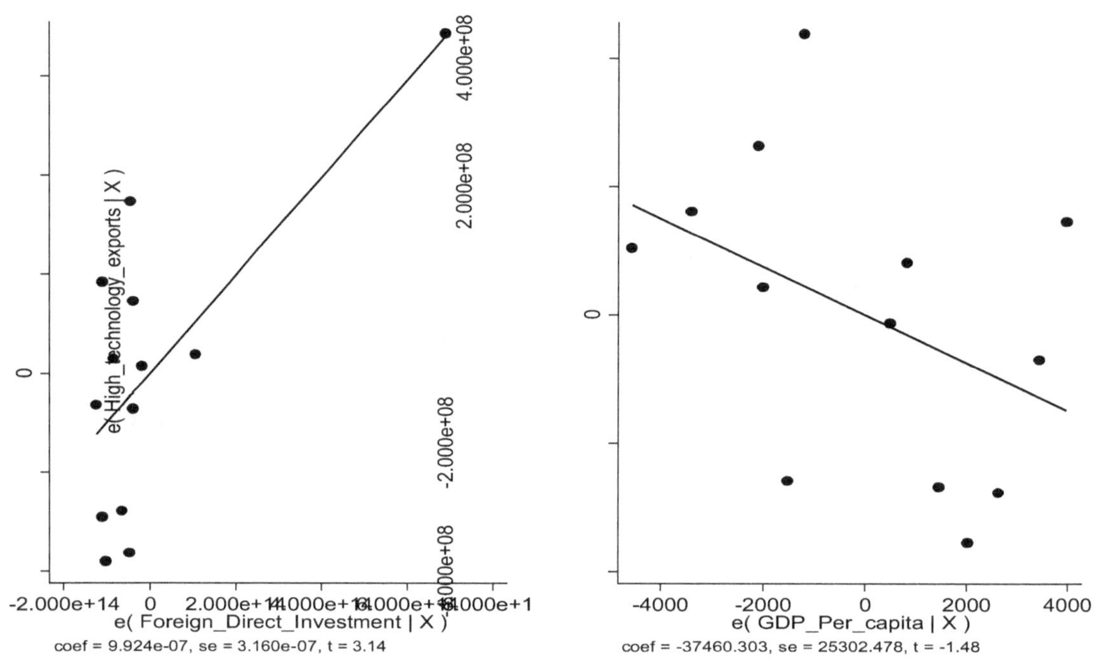

APPENDIX B

MATHEMATICAL ANNEX.

As noted above, Deslandes' equation (1975) for the ratio of operating cost of production P to production capacity C is expressed as follows:

$$\frac{P2}{P1} = \left[\frac{C2}{C1}\right]^{-a} \quad (1)$$

If the final operating cost is cleared, you will have.

$$P2 = P1\left[\frac{C2}{C1}\right]^{-a} \quad (2)$$

If it is considered that the production capacity will be equal to the quantities produced in two different periods, the equation can be expressed by the following equation:

$$P2 = P1\left[\frac{Q2}{Q1}\right]^{-a} \quad (3)$$

Where capacity has been equated with production. Now the quantity produced will be assumed equal to the production capacity.

$$Q = C \quad (4)$$

However, Deslandes' model (1975), introduces an important element, it is a dynamic model, since it implies changes both in the level of production and in the operating cost and the operating costs are a type of cost assumed by the entrepreneur. In such a way that:

$$P = Costs \quad (5)$$

If we substitute in equation (3), we get:

$$Co2 = Co1\left[\frac{Q2}{Q1}\right]^{-a} \quad (6)$$

Where Co, corresponds to the operating costs in different periods. Equation (6) expresses the relationship between operating costs and the level of production, which in Deslandes' model (1975) refers to *production capacity*. Both variables are expressed in two moments that will have or not representative variations, according to the value of the volume factor (-a). In such a way that the equation can be expressed as:

$$Co_t = C_{t-1}\left[\frac{Q_t}{Q_{t-1}}\right]^{-a} \quad (7)$$

Where Co_t and C_{t-1}, express operating costs in different periods. On the other hand, a relationship is established between the cost of equipment and the productive capacity:

$$\frac{Q2}{Q1} = \left[\frac{C2}{C1}\right]^{-b} \quad (8)$$

It can be considered that the equipment refers to the incorporation of *technology* in the productive process, in such a way that the following equivalence can be made:

$$Q = T \quad (9)$$

Where T, refers to the incorporation of said technology in the productive unit, expressed in its monetary value. In this way, the following substitution can be considered in equation (8):

$$\frac{T2}{T1} = \left[\frac{C2}{C1}\right]^{-b} \quad (10)$$

If we substitute, as in the previous case, the production capacity by the production level, we have the following equation:

$$T2 = T1\left[\frac{Q2}{Q1}\right]^{-b} \quad (11)$$

Both variables are also expressed, as in the case of operating costs, as variations in two moments, according to the value of the volume factor, in this case (-b). In such a way that the equation can be expressed as:

$$T_t = T_{t-1}\left[\frac{Q_t}{Q_{t-1}}\right]^{-b} \quad (12)$$

With respect to investment, the explanatory model considers a relationship between levels of production and investment:

$$\frac{I2}{I1} = \left[\frac{C2}{C1}\right]^{f} \quad (13)$$

If the investment is intended to cover the costs of the productive unit, we have then:

$$I = CT \quad (14)$$

Where CT, its total costs. If we substitute (14) in (13), we will have:

$$\frac{CT2}{CT1} = \left[\frac{C2}{C1}\right]^{f} \quad (15)$$

In addition, the production capacity per Q, as in the other two equations, we will have:

$$CT2 = CT1\left[\frac{Q2}{Q1}\right]^{f} \quad (16)$$

If we include the dynamic approach in it, we will have:

$$CT_t = CT_{t-1}\left[\frac{Q_t}{Q_{t-1}}\right]^f \quad (17)$$

The model can be represented by these three equations:

$$Co_t = C_{t-1}\left[\frac{Q_t}{Q_{t-1}}\right]^{-a} \quad (18)$$

$$T_t = T_{t-1}\left[\frac{Q_t}{Q_{t-1}}\right]^{-b} \quad (19)$$

$$CT_t = CT_{t-1}\left[\frac{Q_t}{Q_{t-1}}\right]^f \quad (20)$$

Where:

Co_t = Operating costs for period t.

C_{t-1} = Incorporation in technology for period t.

T_{t-1} = Incorporation in technology for period t.

CT_t = Total costs for period t.

CT_{t-1} = Total costs for period t-1

Q_{t-1} = Production level for the period t-1

Q_t = Production level for period t.

-a = Volume factor for operating costs.

-b = Volume factor for the incorporation of technology.

f = Volume factor for total costs.

Now, if we consider that the total investment will cover the costs of the operating unit, we can consider that this investment is equal to the investment in operating costs and technology:

$$CT_t = Co_t + T_t \quad (21)$$

The entrepreneur can choose the proportion p, of the total investment that can be used to cover operating costs and the proportion *(1-p)*, which will be used to incorporate equipment (technology):

$$CT_t = p[Co_t] + (1-p)[T_t] \quad (22)$$

So, the total costs of a period can be expressed as:

$$CT_t = p\{C_{t-1}\left[\frac{Q_t}{Q_{t-1}}\right]^{-a}\} + (1-p)\{T_{t-1}\left[\frac{Q_t}{Q_{t-1}}\right]^{-b}\} \quad (23)$$

$$CT_t = p\{\frac{C_{t-1}}{\left[\frac{Q_t}{Q_{t-1}}\right]^{a}}\} + (1-p)\{\frac{T_{t-1}}{\left[\frac{Q_t}{Q_{t-1}}\right]^{b}}\} \quad (24)$$

To the extent that the p ratio intended to cover operating costs decreases, the incorporation of soft or hard technology will be greater *(1-p)*.

On the other hand, with the set of equations on production and costs, we can obtain the values of the ***multifactorial capital and labor coefficients***. If we have the Cobb-Douglas function, expressed as:

$$Q = AL^{\alpha}K^{\beta} \quad (1)$$

Where L and K, correspond to the labor force and capital respectively, function that is subject to another isocost function, which as observed, is expressed as follows:

$$C = wL + rK \ (2)^{39}$$

Moreover, there is a cost function:

$$C = CF + CVU * Q \ (3)$$

From equation (2) of *Isocost*, it clears L, we have:

$$L = \frac{C - rK}{w} \quad (4)$$

In addition, if you clear the other factor *(capital)* from the same equation, you get:

$$K = \frac{C - wL}{r} \quad (5)$$

If you replace (3) in (2), you will have it

$$CF + CVU * Q = wL + rK \ (6)$$

If Q clears, we will have:

---

[39] It will be assumed that the financial capital is equal to the total cost, since the productive unit is supposed to employ it in production directly.

$$Q = \frac{wL + rK - CF}{CVU} \quad (7)$$

If we now replace (7) in the Cobb-Douglas function:

$$\frac{wL + rK - CF}{CVU} = AL^{\alpha}K^{\beta} \quad (8)$$

If we clear it now K^{β}, *we will* get*:*

$$\frac{wL + rK - CF}{CVU * AL^{\alpha}} = K^{\beta} \quad (9)$$

If you replace (5) in (9), you get:

$$\frac{wL + r[\frac{C - wL}{r}] - CF}{CVU * AL^{\alpha}} = [\frac{C - wL}{r}]^{\beta} \quad (10)$$

$$\frac{C - CF}{CVU * AL^{\alpha}} = [\frac{C - wL}{r}]^{\beta}$$

$$\frac{CVT}{CVU * AL^{\alpha}} = [\frac{C - wL}{r}]^{\beta}$$

$$Log [\frac{CVT}{CVU * AL^{\alpha}}] = Log [\frac{C - wL}{r}]^{\beta}$$

$$Log [\frac{CVT}{CVU * AL^{\alpha}}] = Log [\frac{C - wL}{r}]^{\beta}$$

$$Log (CVT) - Log (CVU * AL^{\alpha}) = \beta Log [\frac{C - wL}{r}]$$

$$\beta = \frac{Log (CVT) - Log (CVU * AL^{\alpha})}{Log [\frac{C - wL}{r}]} \quad (11)$$

This gives the multifactorial coefficient of capital for the productive unit, which expresses the relationship between productive factors capital *(K)*, labor *(L)*, wages *(w)*, cost of capital *(r)*, fixed costs and variable unit costs:

$$\beta = \frac{Log (CVT) - Log (CVU * AL^{\alpha})}{Log (C - wL) - Log \ r} \quad (12)$$

If we now replace (7) in the Cobb-Douglas function:

$$\frac{wL + rK - CF}{CVU} = AL^{\alpha}K^{\beta} \quad (13)$$

If we clear it now, L^{α} we will get:

$$\frac{wL + rK - CF}{CVU * AK^{\beta}} = L^{\alpha} \quad (14)$$

If you replace (4) in (14), you get it:

$$\frac{w[\frac{C-rK}{W}]+rK-CF}{CVU*AL^{\alpha}} = [\frac{C-rK}{W}]^{\alpha} \quad (15)$$

$$\frac{rK-CF}{CVU*AK^{\beta}} = [\frac{C-rK}{w}]^{\alpha}$$

$$\frac{rK-CF}{CVU*AK^{\beta}} = [\frac{C-rK}{w}]^{\alpha}$$

$$Log\ [\frac{rK-CF}{CVU*AK^{\beta}}] = Log\ [\frac{C-rK}{w}]^{\alpha}$$

$$Log\ [\frac{rK-CF}{CVU*AK^{\beta}}] = Log\ [\frac{C-rK}{w}]^{\alpha}$$

$$Log\ (rK - CF) - Log\ (CVU * AK^{\beta}) = \alpha Log\ [\frac{C-rK}{w}]$$

$$\alpha = \frac{Log\ (rK-CF)\ -\ Log\ (CVU*AK^{\beta})}{Log\ [\frac{C-rK}{w}]} \quad (16)$$

This gives the ***multifactorial coefficient of labor*** for the productive unit, which expresses the relationship between productive factors capital *(K)*, labor *(L)*, wages *(w)*, cost of capital *(r)*, fixed costs, variable unit costs and the ***multifactorial coefficient of capital***

$$\alpha = \frac{Log\ (rK-CF)\ -\ Log\ (CVU*AK^{\beta})}{Log\ (C-rK)-Log\ w} \quad (17)$$

The marginal replacement rate can be expressed as:

$$TMS = \alpha b / \beta a \quad (18)$$

Substituting the factors *K* and *L* into the equation and the multifactorial ***capital-labor coefficients results*** in:

$$TMS = \frac{K*\frac{Log\ (rK-CF)\ -\ Log\ (CVU*AK^{\beta})}{Log\ (C-rK)-Log\ w}}{L*\frac{Log\ (CVT)\ -\ Log\ (CVU*AL^{\alpha})}{Log\ (C-wL)-Log\ r}}$$

$$TMS = \frac{K*[Log\ (rK-CF)-Log\ (CVU*AK^{\beta})]*[Log\ (C-wL)-Log\ r]}{L*[Log\ (C-rK)-Log\ w]*[Log\ (C-rK)-Log\ w]} \quad (19)$$

APPENDIX C

MEAN, STD AND OTHER STATISTICAL VALUES

Variable	Obs	Mean	Std. Dev.	Min	Max
AVERAGE	11	7.754546	11.30312	.01	36.41

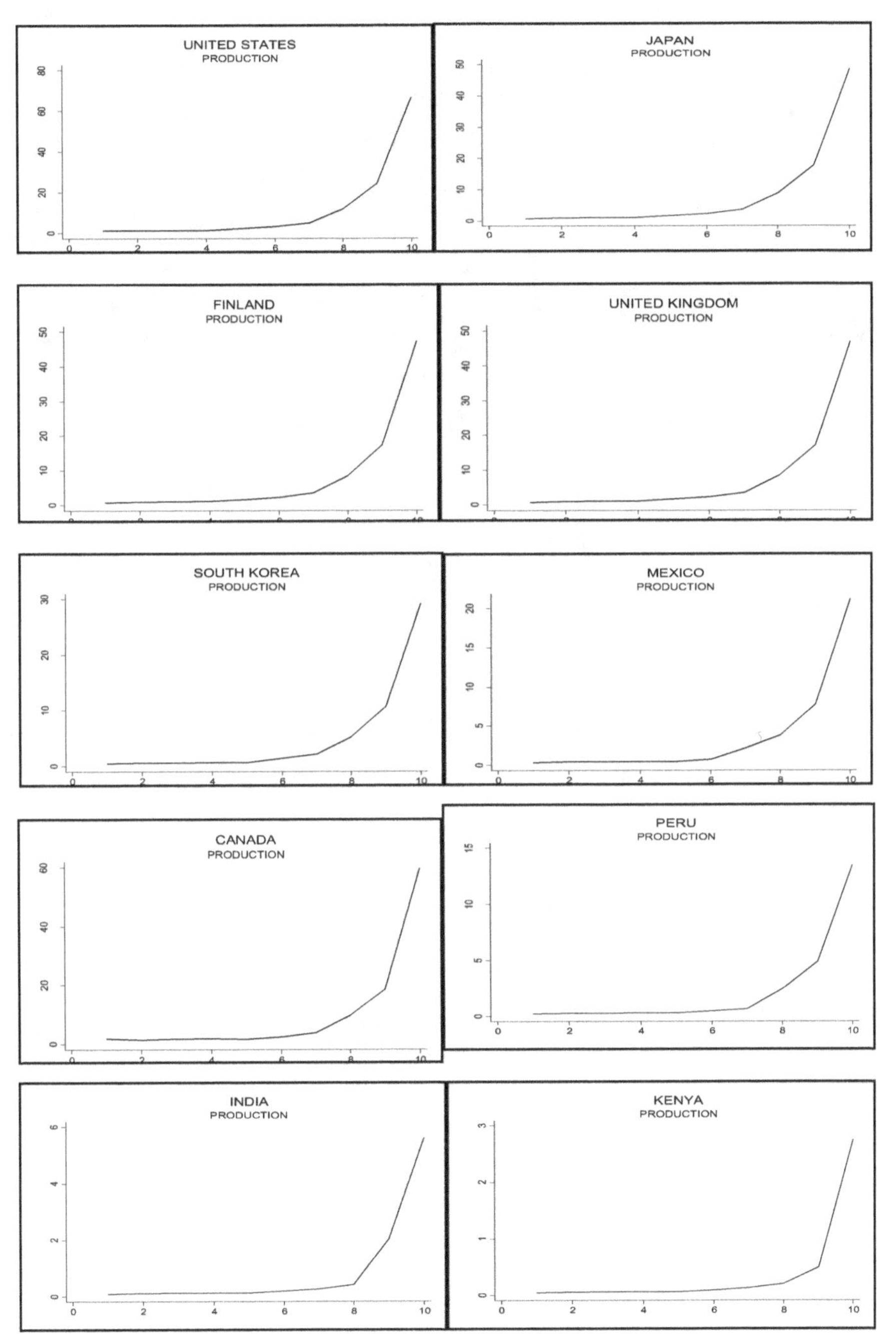

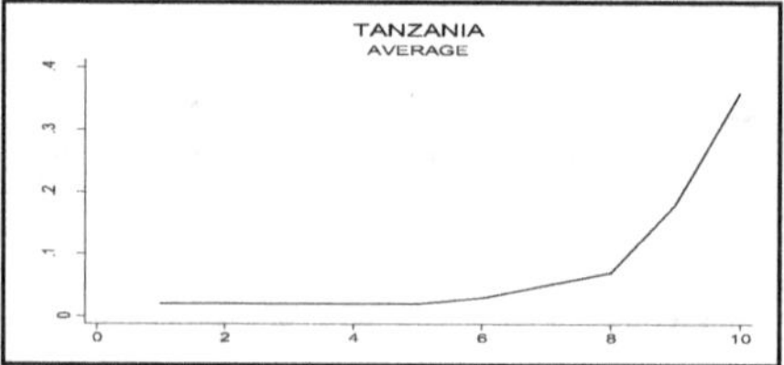

TANZANIA
AVERAGE

APPENDIX 4

BEHAVIOR OF THE COLCAP INDEX 2008-2019

Year 2008.

Variable	Obs	Mean	Std. Dev.	Min	Max
COLCAP	236	915.8525	75.36319	686.65	1032.08

. regress COLCAP DAY

Source	SS	df	MS		
Model	283505.471	1	283505.471	Number of obs = 236	
Residual	1051202.96	234	4492.32035	F(1, 234) = 63.11	
				Prob > F = 0.0000	
				R-squared = 0.2124	
				Adj R-squared = 0.2090	
Total	1334708.43	235	5679.61035	Root MSE = 67.025	

COLCAP	Coef.	Std. Err.	t	P>|t|	[95% Conf. Interval]	
DAY	-.5087533	.0640416	-7.94	0.000	-.634925	-.3825816
_cons	976.1397	8.753687	111.51	0.000	958.8936	993.3858

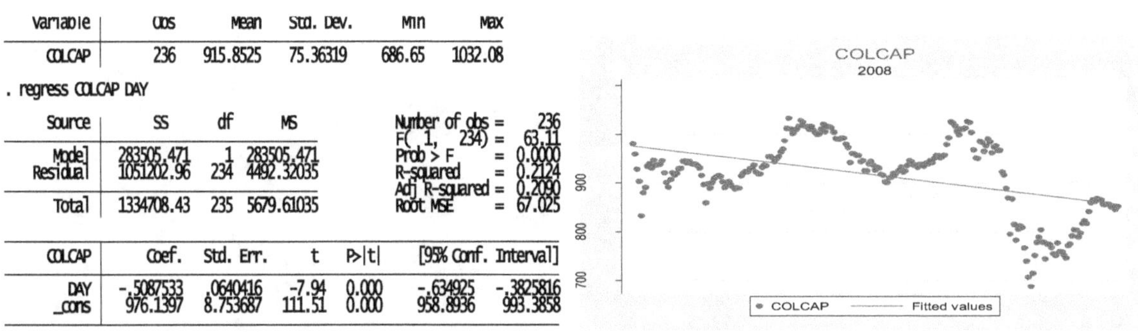

Year 2009

Variable	Obs	Mean	Std. Dev.	Min	Max
COLCAP	242	1089.132	187.4582	825.17	1382.63

. regress COLCAP DAY

Source	SS	df	MS		
Model	8083496.56	1	8083496.56	Number of obs = 242	
Residual	385382.528	240	1605.76053	F(1, 240) = 5034.06	
				Prob > F = 0.0000	
				R-squared = 0.9545	
				Adj R-squared = 0.9543	
Total	8468879.09	241	35140.5771	Root MSE = 40.072	

COLCAP	Coef.	Std. Err.	t	P>|t|	[95% Conf. Interval]	
DAY	2.6162	.0368733	70.95	0.000	2.543563	2.688836
_cons	771.2637	5.167852	149.24	0.000	761.0835	781.4438

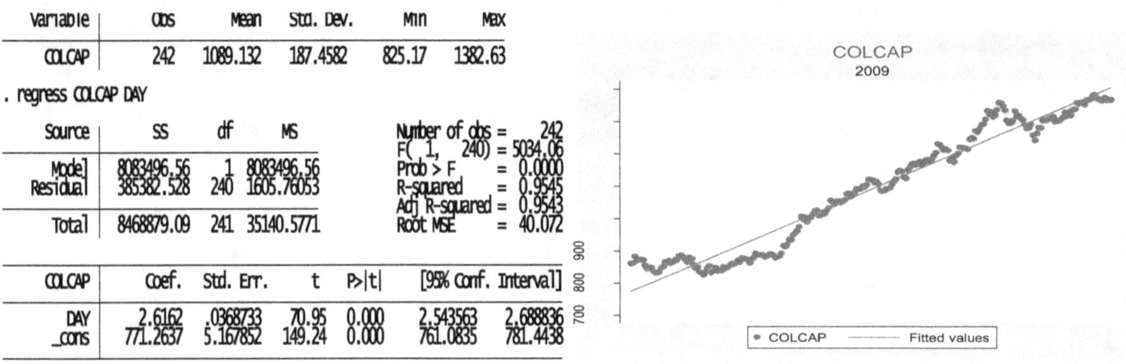

Year 2010.

Variable	Obs	Mean	Std. Dev.	Min	Max
COLCAP	245	1572.887	182.3206	1326.08	1942.37

. regress COLCAP DAY

Source	SS	df	MS		
Model	7124992.49	1	7124992.49	Number of obs = 245	
Residual	985758.7	243	4056.62017	F(1, 243) = 1756.39	
				Prob > F = 0.0000	
				R-squared = 0.8785	
				Adj R-squared = 0.8780	
Total	8110751.19	244	33240.7835	Root MSE = 63.692	

COLCAP	Coef.	Std. Err.	t	P>|t|	[95% Conf. Interval]	
DAY	2.411223	.0575344	41.91	0.000	2.297893	2.524552
_cons	1276.307	8.163191	156.35	0.000	1260.227	1292.387

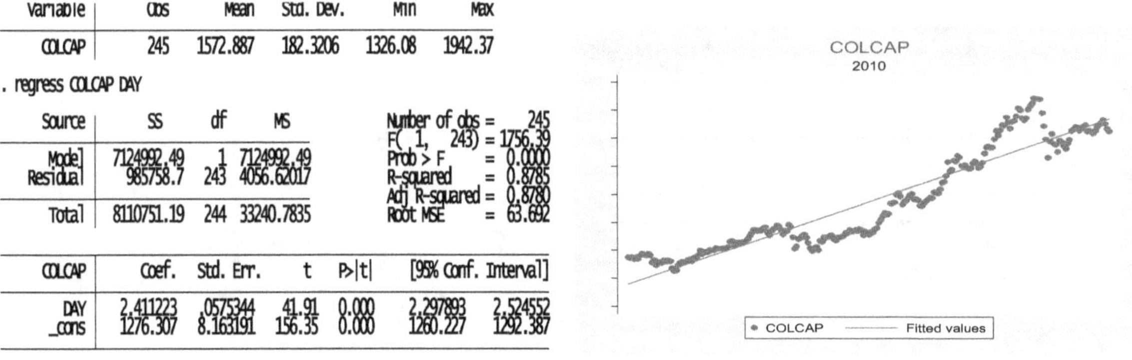

Year 2011.

Variable	Obs	Mean	Std. Dev.	Min	Max
COLCAP	246	1663.034	71.39613	1482.59	1810.27

. regress COLCAP DAY

Source	SS	df	MS		
Model	903127.909	1	903127.909		
Residual	345736.855	244	1416.95433		
Total	1248864.76	245	5097.4072		

Number of obs = 246
F(1, 244) = 637.37
Prob > F = 0.0000
R-squared = 0.7232
Adj R-squared = 0.7220
Root MSE = 37.642

COLCAP	Coef.	Std. Err.	t	P>|t|	[95% Conf. Interval]	
DAY	-.8532301	.0337963	-25.25	0.000	-.9197999	-.7866604
_cons	1768.408	4.814662	367.30	0.000	1758.924	1777.892

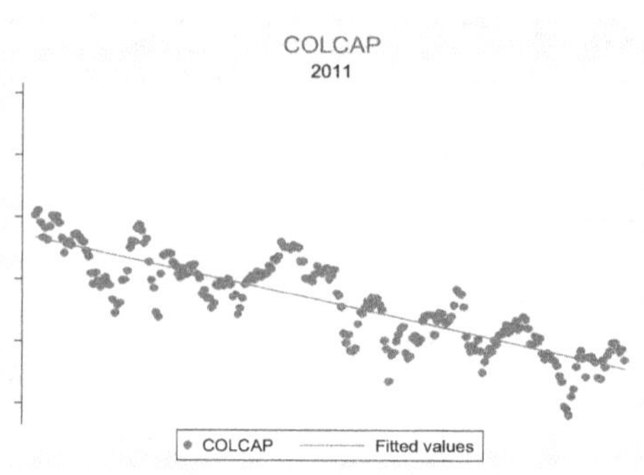

Year 2012.

Variable	Obs	Mean	Std. Dev.	Min	Max
COLCAP	244	1706.615	60.9152	1577.71	1835.82

. regress COLCAP DAY

Source	SS	df	MS		
Model	212426.844	1	212426.844		
Residual	689264.003	242	2848.19836		
Total	901690.848	243	3710.66192		

Number of obs = 244
F(1, 242) = 74.58
Prob > F = 0.0000
R-squared = 0.2356
Adj R-squared = 0.2324
Root MSE = 53.369

COLCAP	Coef.	Std. Err.	t	P>|t|	[95% Conf. Interval]	
DAY	.4189037	.0485059	8.64	0.000	.3233561	.5144514
_cons	1655.299	6.854196	241.50	0.000	1641.798	1668.801

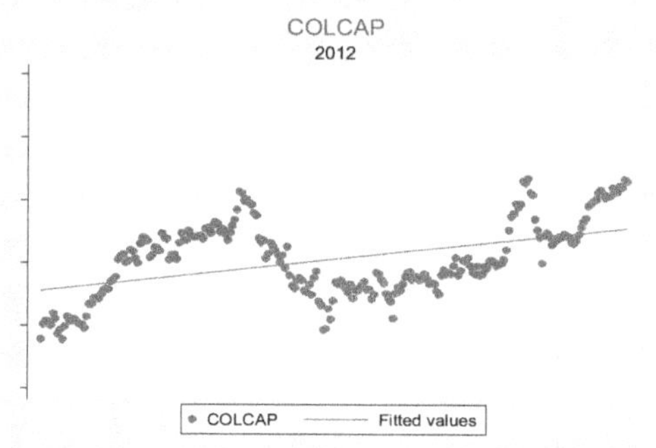

Year 2013.

Variable	Obs	Mean	Std. Dev.	Min	Max
COLCAP	244	1727	81.72673	1550.7	1889.3

. regress COLCAP DAY

Source	SS	df	MS		
Model	594725.195	1	594725.195		
Residual	1028334.41	242	4249.31573		
Total	1623059.6	243	6679.25762		

Number of obs = 244
F(1, 242) = 139.96
Prob > F = 0.0000
R-squared = 0.3664
Adj R-squared = 0.3638
Root MSE = 65.187

COLCAP	Coef.	Std. Err.	t	P>|t|	[95% Conf. Interval]	
DAY	-.7009188	.0592474	-11.83	0.000	-.8176251	-.5842124
_cons	1812.863	8.372032	216.54	0.000	1796.371	1829.354

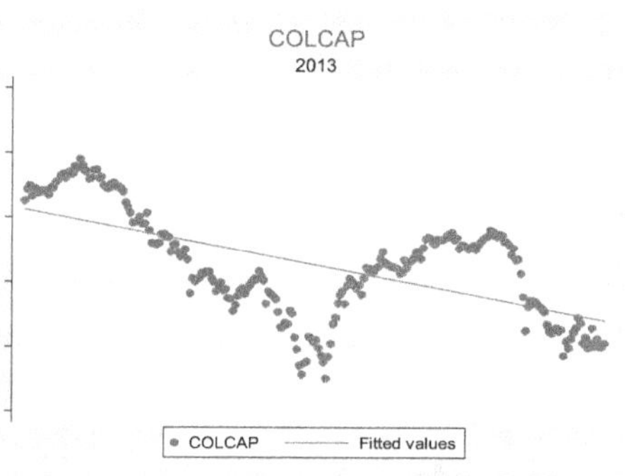

Year 2014.

```
    Variable |       Obs        Mean    Std. Dev.       Min        Max

      COLCAP |       244    1628.697    91.26476    1348.38    1780.25

. regress DAY COLCAP

      Source |       SS           df       MS              Number of obs =     244
                                                           F(  1,   242) =    3.63
       Model |   17898.834         1   17898.834          Prob > F      =  0.0579
    Residual |  1192646.17       242  4928.28994          R-squared     =  0.0148
                                                           Adj R-squared =  0.0107
       Total |   1210545         243  4981.66667          Root MSE      =  70.202

         DAY |     Coef.   Std. Err.      t    P>|t|     [95% Conf. Interval]

      COLCAP |   .0940386   .0493449     1.91   0.058    -.0031616    .1912388
       _cons |  -30.66037   80.49338    -0.38   0.704    -189.2174    127.8967
```

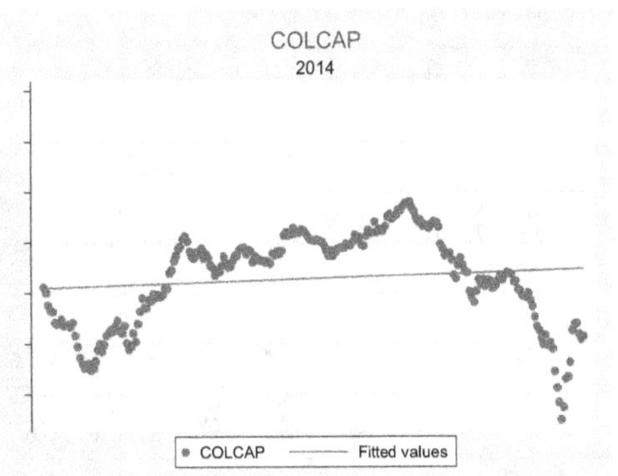

Year 2015.

```
    Variable |       Obs        Mean    Std. Dev.       Min        Max

      COLCAP |       242    1286.869    92.02925    1051.25    1483.89

. regress COLCAP DAY

      Source |       SS           df       MS              Number of obs =     242
                                                           F(  1,   240) =  813.59
       Model |  1576167.04         1  1576167.04          Prob > F      =  0.0000
    Residual |  464954.227       240  1937.30928          R-squared     =  0.7722
                                                           Adj R-squared =  0.7713
       Total |  2041121.27       241  8469.38287          Root MSE      =  44.015

      COLCAP |     Coef.   Std. Err.      t    P>|t|     [95% Conf. Interval]

         DAY |  -1.15524   .0405015    -28.52   0.000    -1.235024   -1.075457
       _cons |   1427.23    5.67635    251.43   0.000     1416.049    1438.412
```

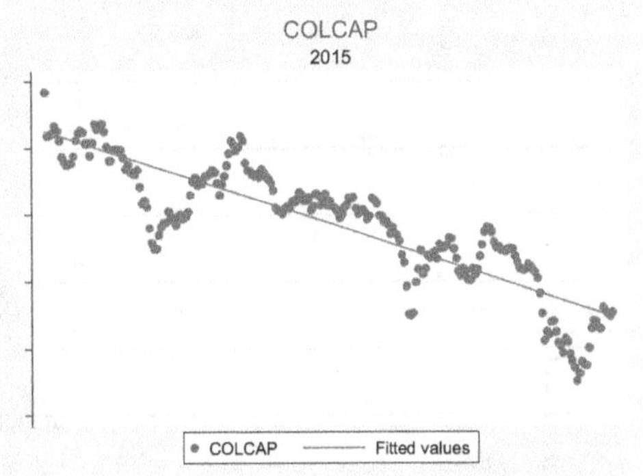

Year 2016.

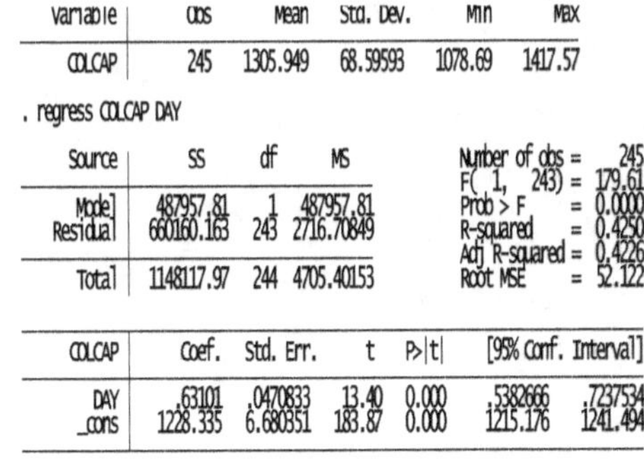

```
    Variable |       Obs        Mean    Std. Dev.       Min        Max

      COLCAP |       245    1305.949    68.59593    1078.69    1417.57

. regress COLCAP DAY

      Source |       SS           df       MS              Number of obs =     245
                                                           F(  1,   243) =  179.61
       Model |   487957.81         1   487957.81          Prob > F      =  0.0000
    Residual |  660160.163       243  2716.70849          R-squared     =  0.4250
                                                           Adj R-squared =  0.4226
       Total |  1148117.97       244  4705.40153          Root MSE      =  52.122

      COLCAP |     Coef.   Std. Err.      t    P>|t|     [95% Conf. Interval]

         DAY |    .63101   .0470833     13.40   0.000     .5382666    .7237534
       _cons |  1228.335   6.680351    183.87   0.000     1215.176    1241.494
```

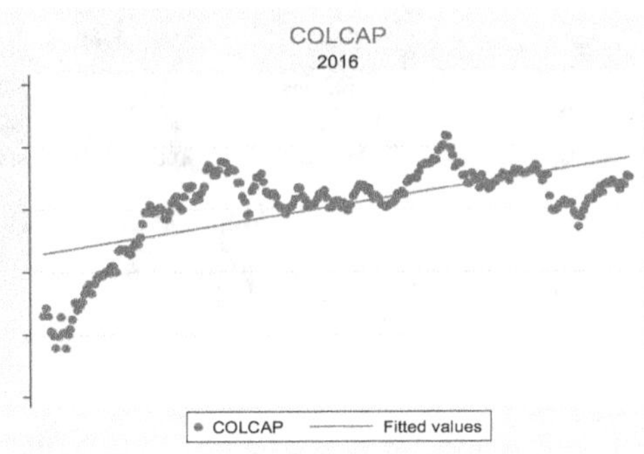

Year 2017.

Variable	Obs	Mean	Std. Dev.	Min	Max
COLCAP	242	1426.846	56.1457	1317.98	1513.65

. regress COLCAP DAY

Source	SS	df	MS
Model	500904.323	1	500904.323
Residual	258809.435	240	1078.37265
Total	759713.759	241	3152.33925

Number of obs = 242
F(1, 240) = 464.50
Prob > F = 0.0000
R-squared = 0.6593
Adj R-squared = 0.6579
Root MSE = 32.839

COLCAP	Coef.	Std. Err.	t	P>|t|	[95% Conf. Interval]	
DAY	.6512514	.0302173	21.55	0.000	.5917264	.7107764
_cons	1347.719	4.235007	318.23	0.000	1339.376	1356.061

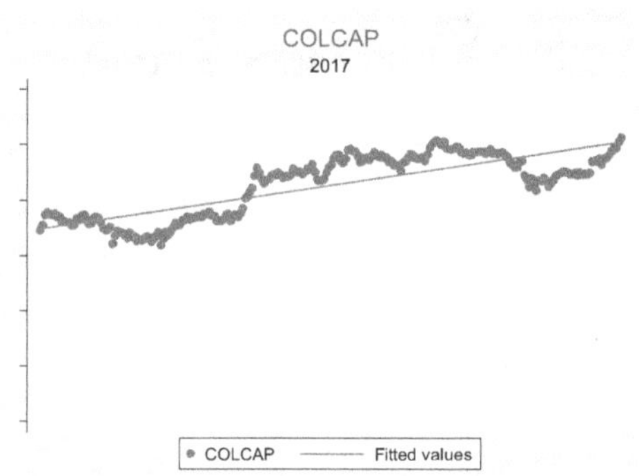

Year 2018.

Variable	Obs	Mean	Std. Dev.	Min	Max
COLCAP	243	1498.023	65.88096	1298.37	1598.4

. regress COLCAP DAY

Source	SS	df	MS
Model	460327.485	1	460327.485
Residual	590025.31	241	2448.2378
Total	1050352.8	242	4340.30081

Number of obs = 243
F(1, 241) = 188.02
Prob > F = 0.0000
R-squared = 0.4383
Adj R-squared = 0.4359
Root MSE = 49.48

COLCAP	Coef.	Std. Err.	t	P>|t|	[95% Conf. Interval]	
DAY	-.6204665	.0452493	-13.71	0.000	-.7096011	-.5313319
_cons	1573.72	6.367889	247.13	0.000	1561.176	1586.264

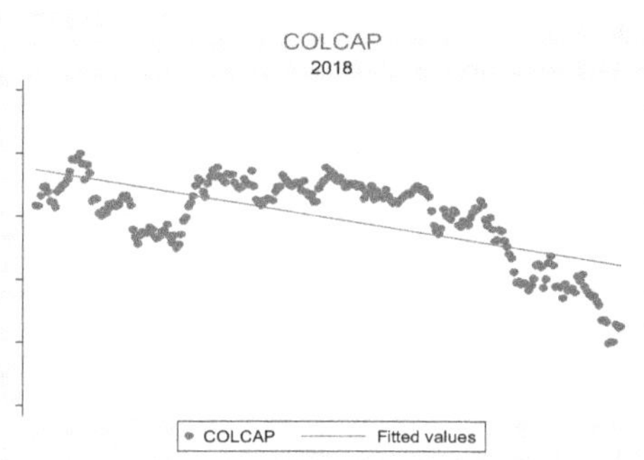

Year 2019.

Variable	Obs	Mean	Std. Dev.	Min	Max
COLCAP	151	1523.816	68.23215	1332.8	1631.3

. regress COLCAP DAY

Source	SS	df	MS
Model	253770.013	1	253770.013
Residual	444573.856	149	2983.71715
Total	698343.868	150	4655.62579

Number of obs = 151
F(1, 149) = 85.05
Prob > F = 0.0000
R-squared = 0.3634
Adj R-squared = 0.3591
Root MSE = 54.623

COLCAP	Coef.	Std. Err.	t	P>|t|	[95% Conf. Interval]	
DAY	.9404915	.1019797	9.22	0.000	.7389784	1.142005
_cons	1452.338	8.934722	162.55	0.000	1434.683	1469.993

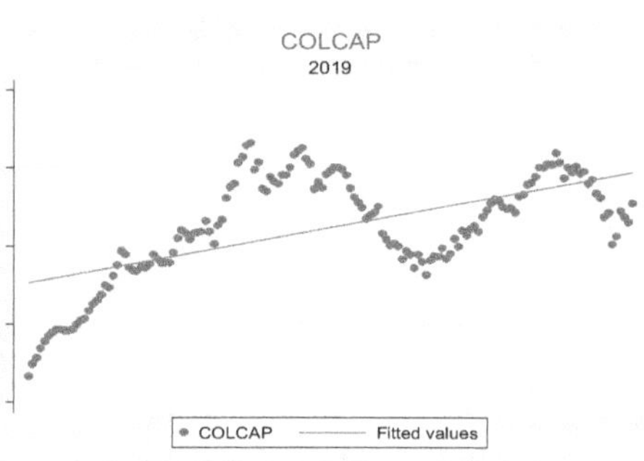

INDEX

****

Economist and psychologist, Master in Social Research, Francisco Jose de Caldas University (Bogota). Phd (candidate) Doctoral studies in History, Philosophy and Heritage of Science and Technology, Universidad Nova de Lisboa. Author of the books: -Productivity and reproduction: Maternity is not a problem. Planning and implementing strategies to achieve permanence in the educational environment of pregnant and lactating women is a social responsibility;- New approach to motherhood: archetype and social representation;- Byzantium, Mali and Russia: some historical aspects about the use of the currency.; -Portfolio theory: an empirical study. Empirical study based on a basket of shares of three companies listed on the Colombian Stock Exchange (BVC). University Professor of some Universities in (Colombia).

This book tries to make an approach between two disciplines: physics and economics, since the application of the preliminaries proposed by physics from the approaches of Paul Dirac (1928). The first chapter focuses on the importance of investment in Latin American countries as a strategy to achieve better levels of innovative incorporation in internal production processes. The document considers it fundamental to analyze the situation of these countries in relation to state and private investment, recognizing that innovation is a complex but significant element in the progress towards overcoming social obstacles such as poverty and the distribution of wealth. The preponderance that MSMEs have currently acquired, as a preferential framework for the economic development of nations and, above all, of the so-called emerging nations, is evidenced by the fact that they have increased significantly in terms of their quantity in the last two decades. The following work try to apply the determinant of the matrices obtained by the physicist to an interaction of two classic productive factors: capital and labor, but not before reviewing the main production functions that have analyzed this relationship. The next chapter make a brief analysis of the theoretical foundations, from the point of view of mathematical statistics of the main models of portfolio emphasizing proposed by Markowitz and an application from a portfolio of three shares of market listed in Colombia during the period between January 2016 and July 2016. The final chapter intends to articulate the usefulness of this function and analyze of the behavior of the shares in the stock market. One may assume that in a daily share price, there may be some impulse events, which will describe specific behavior in discrete periods in a normal or traditional trading market, and the mathematical development of its function, may constitute a tool for the analysis of these motions

ISBN 9798647513168